sanctuary

How One Anxiety-Riddled Mom Built
a Safe Space for Emotional Healing

Cara Baker

PaperTiger.store

Developmental Editing and Writing by Aly Hawkins
Developmental Editing by Shawn Smucker | ShawnSmucker.com
Copyediting by Clare Fernández | ClareFernandez.com
Book Design by Transcendent Publishing | TranscendentPublishing.com
Illustrations by Kira Komarianska
Cover photo by Lauren Napier Photography | LaurenNapierPhotography.com

ISBN: 979-8-9890682-1-0

"All forgiveness must begin by facing the truth."

— Dalai Lama XIV

Table of Contents

Introduction

I am about to share with you some very personal stories from my life, recollections of my past. These narratives serve as milestones of a path I have walked—one marked by challenges, pain, insights, and transformations.

I wrote this book for those who have walked a path like mine. My particular path has been fraught with religious trauma, a lack of essential mental health resources, and the overwhelming burden of caring for a spouse with a terminal illness. These are profoundly challenging experiences. Feeling isolated, lost, and without the guidance we so desperately need takes its toll.

I understand that some family members and friends may find it difficult to read the candid and, at times, painful accounts of the events that have shaped and forever changed my life. You don't have to read this book if you don't want to. I hope that you can recognize my intention to offer support, understanding, and hope to those who have faced or are currently facing similar struggles.

Religious and family trauma can be a crushing weight (especially when bound up together), *and* making peace with your trauma can be an opportunity for personal growth and discovery. Navigating a mental health challenge can feel insurmountable, *and* it can be a lesson in resilience and the power of support (and meds). Watching my children's father suffer a terminal illness was heart-wrenching, *and* it was an experience that transformed me into a stronger, more compassionate individual.

While your journey and its specific stories may sound different, I'd be willing to wager the arc of our life stories are probably similar: innocence, loss of innocence, self-discovery, life's curveballs, and ultimately coming to terms with what life throws at you. All of those ups and downs require grieving, understanding, and compassion.

In my journey, I have encountered people who have been willing to share their own stories, offer guidance, and lend a comforting hand during the darkest of moments.

I hope my story hits home for you and serves as a source of solace and inspiration. And if you're enduring your trials in silence, I hope these pages let you know you're not alone.

In sharing these personal pieces of my life, I will cover the following topics:

- **Examining Beliefs:** I talk about times when I needed to assess my beliefs—how they came to be, how they were tested, and how they evolved. These stories are about discovering who I am, and realizing that what I believe deeply influences how I see and do things.

- **Unpacking the Past:** I revisit key points in my life where I had to face my past. These stories are about tackling tough memories, understanding how they've shaped me, and learning to move forward stronger and wiser.

- **Treating Mental Health as Physical Health:** I share the ups and downs of my mental health journey, and why it's as important as physical health. This part is all about finding a healthy balance, reaching out for help when necessary, and developing habits to keep my mind and emotions in check.

- **Dealing with Life's Curveballs:** I share the deeply personal story of my husband's battle with terminal cancer. Life has a way of throwing us into situations we never anticipated and in no way could ever prepare for. These stories are about finding strength in vulnerability, adapting to new realities, and discovering growth in the midst of heartache.

- **Facing Death to Truly Live:** This is the big one. I share how thinking about death has actually helped me live more fully and authentically. It's about coming to terms with life's temporary nature and making the most of every moment.

As you read this book, remember that my stories are signposts, meant to inspire and guide your path, not dictate it. Your journey is your own, rich with its own lessons and revelations. A friend shared with me a Richard Rohr quote in which he warned that pain that is not transformed gets transmitted.[1] I have found that writing is a great way to process and transform pain. I hope you take away from my story the courage to share your own story.

Just as I walked into my therapist's office years ago, my heart full of cautious hope, I embarked on the journey of writing this book. This process is not just about storytelling; it's about scratching that itch until it no longer demands my attention. It's about mothering myself, about being my own source of comfort, care, safety, and guidance.

In writing these stories, I am not only preserving memories; I am actively engaging in a process of healing and self-acceptance. Perhaps there's a fear, too, a worry that one day I might also lose these precious stories to the fog of forgetfulness. But in writing them down, I make them immortal, etched not just on paper, but in the fabric of my being.

If you are struggling with anxiety, this book is a companion. It's a reminder that you are not alone in the way you feel day-to-day. The stories within these pages can be mirrors reflecting your own struggles and triumphs. I hope they're a testament to the resilience of the human spirit and a guide to finding that inner source of comfort and wholeness. Remember that the path to self-healing and wholeness is ongoing. There's no final destination. Our lives

---

[1] Adapted from Richard Rohr, *A Spring Within Us: A Book of Daily Meditations* (CAC Publishing: 2016), 120-121.

are collections of moments and memories, some clear and some fading. But in accepting them all, we find a path to true peace and fulfillment.

To those who've walked alone, grappling with your own load, I hope that my words offer you a sense of solidarity and the knowledge that you are not your worst moments nor your best. We are connected through the human experience and our capacity to heal and grow— if we choose to be. May you find within these pages the support and guidance that I sought in my darkest hours.

May we all move forward towards the light of hope, resilience, and understanding.

1 A New Beginning

I have a hard time describing my delight when I pull on rain boots and a jacket over my flannel granny gown and wade out into the mud pit to feed my three chickens and collect their beautiful eggs. It feels like some kind of miracle that I'm the first on earth to experience. It's like the internet meme "What Gives People Feelings of Power," and under "money," and "status," the bar graph tops out at "growing a tomato." I could make another bar graph that says, "Collecting eggs from chickens you bought from mypetchicken.com."

Another meme reads: "Growing your own tomatoes is the best way to devote 3 months of your life to saving $2.17." Can I ever relate to that. And yet, it's worth it.

I don't even like tomatoes, and I haven't kept up with how much time or money I've invested into those chickens. But when you move your family to six acres outside the city, there comes an expectation, or at least a curiosity, to try your hand at gardening and keeping a chicken or two.

When we moved into this house last September, a big, overgrown garden sat out front, but I wanted a smaller garden out back. So my neighbor, being neighborly, tilled and leveled the ground so I could sow grass. Rain was on the way that day, so I rushed around in wide-legged yoga pants and flip-flops, trying as quickly as humanly possible—for a human who was not accustomed to this type of work, that is—to get the seed in the ground and covered with hay. I was filthy and sweating from head to toe, pushing this spreader through the bumpy soil as if I had done it a hundred times before (I definitely had not). My friend Isabella snapped a picture, and she and her husband Benjamin, who was there painting the house, got the biggest laugh at my expense. Check out Cara the FARMER.

This was not exactly where I envisioned myself a year prior to this moment. Certainly not thirty years ago. The Cara of my youth wouldn't know what to do with me.

For starters, I am not used to getting my hands dirty. I remember childhood summer vacations spent at my grandmother's house.

She would ask my cousin and me to snap green beans and shuck corn while she canned vegetables in the kitchen. I would recoil at the sight of a bug or worm, and she pointed out that such tasks require you to not be afraid to get dirty. She certainly wasn't. I remember seeing her chase down a blue racer snake and chop its head off with a hoe.

But as gutsy as she was, she could be just as glamorous. She was a pastor's wife, and I marveled at her lavender-printed, wallpapered bedroom and her immaculate closet, which was full of elegant dress suits and leather pumps. A white styrofoam mannequin head sat on her dresser, displaying her backup wig with tiny pearl-topped push pins protruding from the neck. I would run my finger along the dresser and take in the smells of her favorite perfume, seeping its fragrance into the air (if I remember correctly, it was Passion by Elizabeth Taylor) and admiring her collection of pins and brooches. This was the side of my grandma that I most wanted to grow up to be like.

One time, when I was five or six years old, my Sunday school teacher told us to sit crisscross applesauce on the white and gray flecked vinyl floor of the fluorescent-lit classroom for Bible story time. I politely declined and requested a chair to sit in. Not because I was too good to sit on the floor but because I was afraid I'd get in trouble with my mom if I got my dress and spotless white tights dirty. My desire for glamor hinged from a place of seeking security—not attention.

Several years ago, I was chatting with Mom when I recalled how particular I was back then. I reminded her how she used to take me downtown to Vanderbilt University for bougie swim lessons. The instructor would get so frustrated because I didn't want to put my head underwater—not because I was afraid, but because I didn't want to get my hair wet! To my surprise, Mom insisted my girlhood fussiness was almost entirely self-imposed.

It stunned me at the time, but now, I think she was right. For years, I told myself a story about how my mom always wanted me to be neat, clean, and put together, and how I was sure to get in trouble if I messed up something nice she had made or bought. But perhaps my meticulous care about looking right on the outside was really about dressing up all that I feared was wrong on the inside.

I was telling a friend the pristine Sunday school dress story the other day, and he laughed. "For the clean princess to become queen of chicken poop is quite a journey." Yes. Quite a journey. That's the journey I seek to unpack in this space, along with the unexpected turns I took along the way.

Now, as I walk around my big farmhouse, enjoying all the lovely things in it, I think of Mom often—mostly because she bought every nice thing in this house. Her dining table and chairs look like they were made for this dining room, and the big, beautiful black hutch still holds her collection of MacKenzie-Childs enamelware. She collected lots of different things, mostly kitchenware, dishes, and entertaining pieces, which have now been passed down to me.

She always had a beautifully decorated table. No one was allowed to eat there except for special occasions. And then we took everything off and used placemats. So I guess my fussiness wasn't entirely self-imposed?

I don't think of myself as fussy anymore. The last couple of years have trampled any remaining rigidity right out of me. But it's okay because, from my freshly tilled soul, something entirely new is emerging.

A few weeks after my brother Harrison and I moved Mom into a memory care facility, COVID-19 struck, and I barely got to see her. Occasionally, I could have a "window visit," as they called it. We would sit on either side of a glass door, each with a walkie-talkie. She held hers against her ear like a phone and looked off into the distance, chatting pleasantly with somebody who wasn't there and certainly wasn't me. She had so much to say that the somebody on the line couldn't get a word in edgewise. I wish I could have understood what she was saying. Because of her aphasia (when the brain mixes up words), everything came out like a baby mimicking conversation: all inflection, animation, and sweetness—but very little sense.

Lately, she had been calling me her sister. At least she still knew I belonged to her. She would ask about the babies, meaning my kids—to her, they're always "the babies." Rowan was thirteen by then and remembered the way she was before; Emmeline was eight and didn't, really. A few years ago, when we were starting to come to grips with the severity of Mom's dementia, I was driving her around town, and she kept asking about my mother.

"Is your mother still alive? How is she?"

Emmeline was in the back. She must have been six and exclaimed with a giggle, "Nana, you're her mom!"

"I am?" she asked, astonished.

"Yeah, and you're my grandma."

"I am? Well, I knew I loved you."

Those were the bittersweet moments of our new normal.

If you're someone who struggles with anxiety, you may find this scene all too familiar. The feeling of things once solid and dependable now slipping through your fingers can be a source of deep anxiety. But within this story lies a profound lesson—the importance of self-reliance and self-care in the face of life's inevitable changes.

Bad things happen, and so do good things. This unpredictability is the stuff of life, and it's something neither you nor I, nor even my mother, with or without dementia, can control. Embracing this truth is at the heart of finding peace and wholeness. For me, the journey to this understanding began with an itch, a metaphorical one that I could no longer ignore.

I used to call Mom every evening, and we'd catch up on the day. I don't know how long it's been—more than a year and a half at least. My hand still remembers the time and reaches for the phone, even though she doesn't and can't. It's like having an itch in the middle of my back that only someone else can reach. It's funny. Mom always seemed to have a middle-of-the-back itch, and she kept a back scratcher in every room of the house. I forgot to pack one for her move into full-time care, and by the time I remembered, her inexhaustible itch was forgotten along with my name.

Too much has happened in the past eighteen months for her not to know about, even though part of me is grateful for her sake and mine that she doesn't. A bigger part of me wishes I had her ear, shoulder, and unconditional love to help me carry it all. It's hard to imagine what she'd say about my life recently. The mixed blessing of her illness is that finding out isn't an option.

These days—at least during this break in COVID restrictions, and now that Mom has been vaccinated—I lie next to her in her bed, which is just a mattress on the floor because she tripped and fell over the bedframe a couple of times. The walls are yellowed, not in a spring buttercup sort of way, more like dingy hospital walls. Pictures of her two granddaughters hang on those paint-chipped walls.

Picture frames are scattered on end tables, some up and some down because she constantly picks them up to carry around with her. A television sits on a nightstand opposite her mattress, but she doesn't know how to turn it on anymore and doesn't have the attention span or cognitive function to watch it. It must be difficult for someone who used to love watching sports of all kinds, Hallmark movies, and of course, The Weather Channel.

I look at her and wonder how she passes the time when I'm not there. A mini fridge sits unused in the corner, full of chilled bottled water. She forgets that it's there or even how often she should drink. An elegant chest of drawers from her old bedroom anchors the room. It is full of mismatched items she picks up and files away with perceived importance. In one, a half-colored sheet from a group activity, a bent photograph of me and my family, a single sock, a clean adult diaper, and a greeting card addressed to a name I don't recognize.

I put my head on her shoulder and try to remember what life was like before. She tells me she loves me, then asks me what I do.

"For a living?"

"Yes," she says.

"I'm a writer."

She pivots her head and looks at me with surprise and delight. "I'm so proud of you," she says.

"I'm proud of you too, Mom."

The morning sun shoots beams of gold on the pile of firewood at the end of the driveway. Now that green fills the trees, porch sitting has become my favorite. I sit wrapped in a gray cardigan that's as oversized as my coffee, my dog nearby with wet paws from his romp in the dewy grass. The wetness hangs in the air, making the world feel more tangible. This is the only time of day when the birds are so alive with song it sounds like a recording of the rainforest. This is my reward for being awake early.

I sit in my chair, reminding myself to relax, to let go of the tension in my body. Pleasure is okay. I'm safe and at home in my body, in my space, and in my life. I'm living in the same book, but I'm beginning a new chapter. There's more to write.

As I sip my coffee, the warmth of the cup seeps into my hands, a comforting embrace. The steam rises, mingling with the cool morning air, creating a dance of mist and light. I close my eyes for a moment, taking in the symphony of nature around me—the chirping of the birds, the gentle rustling of leaves, and the distant bark of a neighbor's dog. It's moments like these that I find myself most reflective, most at peace.

I glance at my dog, now contentedly dozing at my feet, and grin. He sighs, unburdened by the complexities of human thought and emotion. I envy him that simplicity, that ability to just be.

Looking back to the canopy trees that line the back of the property covering the creek bed, I think about the journey ahead. It's one of healing, understanding, and, most importantly, acceptance—acceptance of my past, my beliefs, and the myriad contradictions that make up who I am.

I take another sip of my coffee, now lukewarm, and set the cup down. It's time to start writing this new chapter, to explore the depths of my experiences and the lessons I can learn from them. There's a story here, one of faith and doubt, of fear and courage, and of the never-ending search for understanding and peace.

I stand up, stretching and feeling a renewed sense of purpose. The path ahead is unclear, but that's okay. I have faith, not just in a higher power, but in myself and the path I'm on. With each step, I'm learning, growing, and finding my way to a place of sanctuary within.

LET'S CHECK IN

If you find reciting daily mantras helpful, consider these as a springboard to write your own:

"I give myself permission to explore and redefine my beliefs."

Allow yourself the freedom to question, explore, and redefine your faith. You may find it deepens when enriched with new perspectives.

"I cultivate gratitude for every step of my journey."

Practice gratitude for both the challenges and joys you encounter, as each contributes to your growth.

"I am resilient, capable of managing fears and anxieties."

Affirm your resilience and ability to face the challenges life presents.

2

Examining Beliefs

*"That's what learning is all about where spirituality is
concerned: unlearning, unlearning almost everything
you've been taught."*

— Anthony de Mello

When I first heard the term "deconstruction," it instantly resonated. While it may sound like a trendy buzzword for millennials and Gen X who are questioning their faith, I know all too well that the process of deconstructing one's beliefs is a deeply personal and often painful one. It's a journey that requires you to confront the belief systems that have defined you for as long as you can remember, and to question whether they still hold weight in your life.

For me, this meant acknowledging the fear and guilt that had been instilled in me from a young age, and learning to navigate a world outside of the strict boundaries of religious doctrine. It's been a journey of self-discovery, and while I still have a long way to go to rebuild, I'm starting to find peace in the redefinition of my beliefs and identity. My hope is the stories in this chapter feel both intimate and universal and help you explore your own beliefs and upbringing with curiosity and compassion.

If you've never seen The Lone Bellow live, you owe it to yourself to experience one of their concerts. It's as if they are there to admire the audience and not the other way around. Their harmonies, big anthemic choruses, and boot-stomping rhythms remind me of Pentecostal church services. Everybody's standing, clapping, singing, waving their hands in the air at some presence or ideal that's bigger than themselves—just like in church. This collective experience transports you to a realm where you can put down what's heavy, connect with a spirit of community, and leave lighter than when you came.

That's probably the only part I miss about my church upbringing.

My mind wanders back to my childhood, to the small, close-knit community where I grew up. I remember the vibrant hymns, the fervent prayers, and the sense of belonging that came from being part of something greater than myself. Those were simpler times, or so they seemed.

Our lives revolved around the church, a simple white brick building with yellow stained glass windows that painted the pews in a nostalgic light during the long Sunday morning services. My family was deeply religious, and faith was the cornerstone of our existence.

It wasn't just going to church eight days a week that made us Apostolic Pentecostal. Church was the single most important part of our lives, and my family was there any time the doors were open: Sunday morning, Sunday night, Wednesday night prayer service, choir practice, weeklong nightly revival meetings, ladies auxiliary meetings, special events. Given that we lived half an hour away from those church doors, our always-there faithfulness was no small thing. Sacrificing sleep on a school night while keeping up with homework was just part of the devotion as a Jesus-only disciple (like members of The Church of Jesus Christ of Latter-day Saints, we didn't believe in the Trinity). And if revival broke out, that took priority over all other activities. And it goes without saying that a young, single person would only date within the church.

It wasn't just a belief system; it was a way of life.

The Bible told us that we were a peculiar people. We did our best to live up to the moniker, although much of our collective peculiarity "as a people" fell on girls and women. No pants, shorts, or skirts above midcalf. No makeup. No jewelry (outside of a wedding ring) or tattoos. No cutting or trimming our hair. Etcetera, ad infinitum. Rules extended to what we listened to (no secular music), watched (no movie theaters or R-rated movies), and participated in (no sports because those are for boys, no cheerleading because of the short skirt, and no high school marching band because of the pants uniform).

Given what I just shared, you might be surprised to hear that I loved the church. Well. A big part of me loved it. I certainly embraced it. But there was a hidden, quiet, unnamed part that was scared spitless, mainly because eschatology—basically the study of the end of times—was (and still is) an absolute obsession in the church: The End of Days, the Rapture, Seven Years of Tribulation, Zionism, the Mark of the Beast. We were suspicious of formal education, but searching the scriptures and seeing "the signs" was another matter entirely. That was information that could literally save your life.

There was so much I genuinely loved about being born into "Apostolic royalty." When we'd visit Papaw's church 250 miles away, where he was the pastor, we were venerated like saintly rock stars. Even in our congregation back home, we were beloved and respected. Everybody knew who I was. Borrowed fame agreed with me: I shone and swelled in that warm and sticky web of deferential friends and admiring acquaintances. But I didn't rest on our family's laurels, either. From early on, I was determined to live up to or surpass the standards set by the Pentecostal aristocracy who ruled my world.

I needed to be baptized in Jesus' name only, but I couldn't do that until I had repented of my sins. There was an order to follow as outlined in the most popular scripture in every sermon: Acts 2:38, where the disciple Peter says to repent, be baptized, and then filled with the Spirit (that last part they took quite literally to mean speaking in tongues). The urge to repent was strong in my seven-year-old body and spirit, but I was also wary of faking it. Why, anything less than whole-hearted contrition would be worse than none at all. Blaspheming the Holy Ghost—though I was unclear on what made this sin so unforgivable—weighed heavy on my mind.

Finally, one Sunday night when Brother Baton (all our ministers were male and called "Brother"—unless they had graduated to "Bishop") was several minutes into his altar call, I broke at last. I beelined straight to the altar, weeping and remorseful, to kneel and plead Jesus' blood over my sin-filled soul. I was immediately surrounded by a host of adult believers, including Mom, praying with me and for me as I confessed my many sins. They all interceded aloud, mostly in the heavenly language, but some in English. We were all caught up in the Spirit together, riding waves of emotion to wherever Jesus decided to take us. When I eventually peeled myself off that altar, I was a little concerned about having not spoken in tongues, which would've been comforting confirmation that I was saved. But mostly, I felt relieved and excited at the prospect of getting baptized.

It went without saying that not just any pastor should baptize someone of my pedigree. We would make a trip to East Tennessee for Papaw to do the honors. I remember going alone into his big office so he could verify my salvation experience for himself by asking a few questions to gauge my understanding. Shortly after, I stepped into the frigid baptismal tank at the front of the sanctuary, teeth chattering from cold and excitement. Gosh, I felt special. So very special. Especially wearing double French braids and a new raspberry taffeta dress.

The cleansing of my sins provided only momentary relief. I was still on step two of three when it came to eternal salvation. The next phase was more challenging, a fact that worried me. Why did speaking in tongues—the only satisfactory evidence of the Spirit's indwelling—come so hard to me? Shouldn't it just ... happen? I can't count the hours I spent draped across various altars, begging for the gift of speaking in an unknown tongue. The adults at our church prayed loudly and tirelessly for me to receive it, and a few kind souls even coached me. What it came down to was this: I *could* speak in tongues (the first time it happened, I was nine) but only when I got emotionally hysterical. That was the key. The problem was that total emotional abandonment is really hard to work up to and a bit scary.

But I was committed. The part of me that loved the church *loved* it—truly, madly, and deeply. There were rules, and I knew how to follow them. I knew my role, and I knew what to do to fit in. It was my identity. I belonged.

But beneath that sense of community and faith, there were undercurrents of fear and uncertainty. The teachings of the church, while rooted in love and salvation, also spoke of judgment and an impending end of days. As a child, those concepts were more than just theological ideas; they were real, looming possibilities that colored my view of the world.

Growing up, I always felt a tug-of-war within me. On one side, there was the comfort and security of my faith and the community. On the other, there was a growing sense of unease, a feeling that all was not as it seemed. Questions began to form in my mind—ones I lined countless notebooks with—that I dared not voice for fear of judgment or retribution.

As the years passed, those questions grew louder, more insistent. They followed me through my teenage years and into adulthood, a constant whisper in the back of my mind. I began to see the world outside our community, a world full of different beliefs, ideas, and perspectives. It was both exhilarating and terrifying.

My journey of self-discovery led me down paths I didn't expect. Each encounter, each book, each conversation opened my eyes a little more. But it would be years before I would begin to understand that my anxiety, the tension that I carried in my body, was not just a personal failing or a lack of faith. It was, in part, the byproduct of a lifetime of strict doctrine, of black-and-white thinking, and of an unspoken fear of what lay outside the familiar walls of my church and community.

Experiences like these, stemming from our family of origin and religious background, contribute to the tapestry of our adult lives, often weaving anxiety into our very being—like a yarn bombing, a form of street art where colorful knit or crochet pieces are placed on public objects like trees, sculptures, or lampposts. While the details of your church upbringing may look different, it likely contains some of the same ingredients. Control, coercion, and a deep-seated need for approval likely sound familiar to you. These elements, common in many religious upbringings, can create a foundation of fear and uncertainty that persists into adulthood.

Control can instill a sense of constant vigilance and the fear of stepping out of line. It's often manifested in rigid guidelines and expectations. Coercion is subtly enforced through communal pressures and expectations. It may lead to a life lived according to others' standards rather than your own. The insatiable quest for approval, particularly from religious or familial authorities, can create a relentless inner critic. You may begin to question your worth and decisions—especially if you're a woman.

As adults, these threads of control, coercion, and the need for approval can manifest in various ways. Do you have perfectionistic or people-pleasing tendencies? What about fear of judgment—or as I describe it, fear of "getting in trouble"? You may have difficulty with boundaries or chronic anxiety (*raises hand*). Addressing these deep-seated issues requires patience and self-compassion. By acknowledging the influence of your upbringing and actively working towards healing, you can create a life that is true to you feeling whole. You learn not to chase the approval of the shifting tides of human judgment.

Our childhoods are the tender time in which our personalities and coping mechanisms are formed. For those raised in environments with rigid religious doctrines, like the fundamentalist community, this shaping and molding is even more pronounced. The rules, the rituals, and the intense focus on spirituality don't just shape beliefs; they sculpt emotional responses and perceptions of the world.

Consider the impact of growing up in a world where every aspect of life, from the clothes you wear to the media you consume, is judged and controlled. Such strict regulation can instill a sense of order and belonging. It also has the potential to spiral into feelings of inferiority. In these environments, the concept of sin and punishment is often emphasized more than that of love and forgiveness. At the very least, the latter comes with conditions.

The fear and constant vigilance of not living up to the community's standards, of committing a sin unknowingly, of failing to experience spiritual milestones as expected—that's a heavy weight to bear. It becomes ingrained, a part of your psyche that you carry into adulthood.

This overarching theme of control inevitably leads to some level of being sheltered. Growing up in a fundamentalist family often means limited exposure to diverse perspectives and experiences. This sheltering can lead to a heightened sense of unfamiliarity and discomfort when encountering different ways of life or belief systems in adulthood. Such encounters can also trigger anxiety as they challenge core beliefs and values ingrained since childhood.

If any of this rings true for you in any way, it's important to acknowledge how these early experiences have influenced your current beliefs and behaviors. Whether it's a religious upbringing, family dynamics, or cultural norms, recognizing their impact is the first step towards understanding and managing the anxiety they may have instilled.

The most important thing to know is that it's okay to have conflicting emotions about your past. You can be grateful for the sense of community and belonging while also recognizing the stress and anxiety it may have caused. My therapist helped me see and appreciate that both can be true.

Take time to think about how your upbringing has shaped you. Be kind to yourself as you unpack these complex emotions. Understand that it's normal to struggle with aspects of your past.

Megan Von Fricken, LCSW, is a self-described exvangelical therapist specializing in religious trauma and cult recovery, empowering individuals to heal from childhood wounds tied to their religious upbringing. You can find her on Instagram **@reclaimingself.therapy**

If you're a parent, I highly recommend checking out Cindy Wang Brandt for resources to help you navigate parenting life and a community that is supportive and welcoming. You can find her at **cindywangbrandt.com**

I didn't want the fire-and-brimstone life for my kids at all. I didn't even want to go to the same type of church I grew up in. Exposing my kids to the same experiences that caused my trauma was a big hell no. The celebrated escapism theology among the churchgoers I grew up around was no joke. The rapture was something to be celebrated: those who are saved are taken to heaven, and those who are left behind must endure Armageddon.

This terrified me as a child and brought about quite a lot of rage and sadness in me as an adult. And when I had kids? Let me be crystal clear: I never, ever want my babies to lie awake, frantically praying not to be abandoned by a family so eager to meet Jesus that they'd leave them behind to fend for themselves in a world about to burn. I would not stand for that fearmongering mentality.

I know a lot of sincerity exists among those who try to panic people out of damnation. I don't think they're malicious—at least not most of them, most of the time. It's an effective psychological trigger.

They really believe they're warning people away from eternal torment in the literal fires of perdition. It lends the task a sense of urgency. I get that. But my understanding of life and death as a reasonable adult now coexists with some not-inconsiderable PTSD.

To grow up in perpetual fear of hell is itself a kind of hell. All it takes is a reference to a microchip, New World Order, or red heifer (an end-of-times prophecy), and I begin to spiral. The thought of my children experiencing the same fear and anxiety that haunted my childhood is unbearable. I want to offer them a world of love, understanding, and acceptance, not one overshadowed by the threat of eternal damnation.

I guess you can say my journey has been as much about unlearning as it has been about learning.

I read a book recommended by a friend called *Awareness* by Father Anthony de Mello. In it, he observes that people who are most preoccupied with life after death aren't living. That was certainly true for me. When I began to learn about anxiety, I discovered that it happens when you live in your head about the future. The antidote is to stay firmly planted in the present moment. And to get there, I had to unpack my past.

Addressing my anxiety required me to confront my fears head-on. It was a process that my body and mind demanded, a path to reclaiming a part of myself that anxiety had stolen. This journey was not just about finding new beliefs; it was a process of healing and coming back to myself.

For many, adulthood brings about an unlearning of deeply rooted beliefs from childhood. This process can be unsettling. It often involves questioning fundamental aspects of your identity and worldview. It might involve grappling with feelings of guilt for stepping away from a religious community. It can certainly spark anxiety over losing the sense of belonging provided by the community.

It's important to recognize that this journey is not about discarding your past but about understanding its influence on your present. Acknowledging the roots of your anxiety is the first step in managing it. Look for a balance between the values you were raised with and the personal beliefs you have developed as an independent adult. This process is not a betrayal of your past but an embrace of personal growth and self-discovery. Most of all, it's about finding peace within yourself.

As I transitioned into adulthood, the sense of belonging and identity I once found within the church began to fade. I was propelled into a quest for a new framework of understanding. This journey led me to explore avenues that were once forbidden in my childhood, such as astrology and the Enneagram. Were these explorations an act of rebellion? Probably. More importantly, they were a search for a deeper understanding of myself and the universe around me.

Astrology, with its focus on celestial patterns and personal destinies, presented a stark contrast to the strict doctrines of my upbringing. It offered a sense of connection to a larger, more mystical world. It felt good to be free from the rigid boundaries of American Christian values that I grew up with. I learned that fortune is not just a blessing from above but a cosmic alignment, a different kind of divine orchestration.

The Enneagram provided a framework for understanding the underlying motivations and needs that shape our personalities. I gained insights into my actions and decisions, both past and present. It was an enlightening perspective on human behavior. I'm a Type Six, identified by a quest for security and a tendency toward anxiety. And I recognized a lifelong pattern. Seeking safety and assurance from authority figures and institutions was my crutch.

These new beliefs and practices did not seek to instill fear or demand blind obedience. This was a stark contrast—and a breath of fresh air—to the teachings presented in my childhood. They encouraged introspection, self-awareness, and a sense of agency. They provided a space where my questions and doubts were not only allowed but encouraged. They offered valuable insights and a sense of connection to something greater.

As I continued on my path, I realized that my evolution required me to step beyond even these frameworks. Astrology and the Enneagram, while enriching, began to feel like stepping stones rather than destinations. They offered a language to understand myself and the world, but I found myself yearning for a deeper, more direct connection with my inner truth.

A realization dawned on me. These systems, much like the religious doctrines of my childhood, are external structures. I used them as substitutions for the very big void I was experiencing. Relying too heavily on them could limit my understanding of the boundless nature of self.

The process of moving beyond these practices was not abrupt, nor was it a rejection of their value. Instead, it was an acknowledgment that my growth required me to trust more in my inner wisdom and less in external systems. The journey was about more than finding new beliefs; it was about redefining my relationship with fear and authority. This shift was not easy; it meant letting go of the comfort and security these systems provided. It meant facing the uncertainty of forging my own path without a predefined map.

As I distanced myself from these practices, I noticed a shift in my perspective. I began to see spirituality not as something to be defined or confined by specific practices but as an ever-evolving, deeply personal journey. I recognized that my spirituality was not separate from me; it was an intrinsic part of my being, as natural and essential as breathing. This awareness felt empowering. It allowed me to embrace a more fluid and expansive view of spirituality, one that adapts and grows. It helped me understand that true wisdom and peace are the goals, not rituals and practices. That's not to say those aren't important, either. In fact, they're helpful tools to express spirituality and center us in our faith.

Remember that your journey of self-discovery is uniquely yours. The paths we take to find our peace and understanding may differ, but the underlying goal is the same. Whether it's exploring new belief systems, redefining old ones, or simply seeking a deeper

understanding of ourselves, the journey is about finding what resonates with our souls.

Your experiences, particularly those rooted in childhood and religious upbringing, play a significant role in shaping your adult life.
As you move forward, embrace the notion that you are not defined
by your past or the beliefs you were raised with. You have the power
to choose your path, seek truth, and find peace in your own understanding of the world. Your journey is about finding balance, healing, and ultimately, a sense of wholeness that resonates with the
deepest parts of who you are.

LET'S CHECK IN

I know sometimes, in my journey, I need a sense of "permission" to
get the help and resources I need. If you're similar, consider this as
me giving you permission to do the following to help you deal with
religious trauma:

Self-reflection: Spend time reflecting on how patterns of anxiety
manifest in your life. Journaling or talking with a trusted friend or
therapist can be helpful.

Challenge old beliefs: Question the beliefs instilled in your childhood. Are they truly yours, or were they imposed upon you?

Cultivate self-acceptance: Practice accepting yourself as you are,
imperfections and all. Understand that your worth is not contin-
gent on others' approval.

Set boundaries: Learn to say no and set limits. It's okay to prioritize your needs and well-being. If this means saying no to a church invitation from your family member that feels unsafe, so be it.

Seek supportive relationships: Surround yourself with people who value and respect you for who you are, not just for what you can do for them.

Practice mindfulness: Mindfulness can help you stay grounded in the present moment and reduce anxiety. Consider keeping a smooth stone in your pocket to rub and help you connect with the present.

Reclaim your autonomy: Make decisions based on your values and desires rather than out of fear or the need to please others.

Embrace your journey: Recognize that personal growth is a life-long journey and celebrate the progress you make. You are not who you were five minutes ago, let alone five years ago.

Explore new belief systems: If your religious background is a source of anxiety, explore other belief systems or spiritual practices that resonate with you.

Seek professional help: If these issues significantly impact your life, consider seeking help from a mental health professional. BetterHelp.com is a good starting resource.

Remember, you have the power to rewrite your story.

Take some time to journal on the following topics. Choose what resonates most with you, and reflect on how and where you can make shifts for the better. You can come back to this section whenever you need prompts to help guide you on your journey.

Childhood beliefs: Think about the core beliefs you were taught in your childhood. Pick one. How has this particular belief influenced your view of the world and yourself?

Sense of community: Reflect on the sense of community you experienced in your religious upbringing. Did you feel supported, pressured to conform—or both?

Fear and control: Were there aspects of your religious upbringing that instilled fear or a sense of control over your actions and thoughts—or body? How do these elements manifest in your life today?

Questioning beliefs: Have you ever found yourself questioning the beliefs you were raised with? What prompted these questions, and how did you handle them?

Exploring new beliefs: Have you explored beliefs or practices outside of your childhood religion? What prompted this exploration, and what have you learned?

Inner conflict: Have you experienced inner conflict between your personal beliefs and the teachings of your childhood religion? How do you navigate this conflict?

Emotional health and well-being: How has your upbringing impacted your emotional health and well-being? Do you notice any patterns of anxiety, guilt, or other emotions that might be linked to this upbringing?

3 | Unpacking the Past

"For those of us lucky enough to live the American Dream, the demons of the life we left behind continue to chase us."

— **J.D. Vance,** *Hillbilly Elegy: A Memoir of a Family and Culture in Crisis*

Reading *Hillbilly Elegy* by J.D. Vance (before he was canceled) opened my eyes to the concept of Adverse Childhood Experiences (ACEs) and their deep connection to trauma and anxiety. This book resonated with my own experiences, illuminating how childhood trauma casts long shadows over our adult lives. It helped me understand that the fears and anxieties I faced were not just emotional responses but were deeply rooted in my early experiences.

This revelation was a pivotal moment in my journey, and it can be for you as well. It allowed me to view my past through a new lens, acknowledging the impact of my childhood experiences on my mental health and well-being. The following are some stories that illustrate what I mean by that.

It's one thing to be a small child, hiding behind a large armchair in your formal living room because you're scared your dad is mad and might hit you. It's another thing to be in your early thirties with a small child yourself, crying and praying with your head buried in your living room couch because Barack Obama was just elected President of the United States, and your church told you that the End Times were just ushered in, so buckle up, buttercup.

The fear was not insignificant; it was a profound and paralyzing force in my life.

I should interject here that my dad never hit me. He hit my brother. Mom and I didn't know at the time, though. She swears if she'd known it was happening, she would have packed up, and we would have left him for good. I believe her, but that knowledge complicated my grief after Dad died when I was an adult. My brother didn't tell us until four months after he passed, and as complex as my relationship with Dad was, this added a new wrinkle.

Dad had a rough childhood and left home in his early teens. After meeting Mom in his twenties, they moved to Nashville in 1969 so he could attend art school. Mom was a first-year teacher in a district that was reintroducing desegregation. It was also the year of Wood-stock and the moon landing. I once asked her if she knew she was living in historic times. She said she didn't. It was everyday life, and while the happenings seemed significant, it never occurred to her how the world was shifting.

Nashville was where they would work and build our family over the next forty years. My father lost his job during the early '90s recession, an event that marked the beginning of a severe depression. He was an old-school graphic artist who cut his teeth using analog design skills. But after the recession, everything transitioned to computers. He couldn't catch up or start over. He lost his career. I was just a kid in high school and couldn't understand. His struggle with this mental illness profoundly impacted our family. I got angry at his anger, I withdrew from his withdrawal, and I gave his silence the silent treatment. In retrospect, there had always been anger, withdrawal, and silence enveloping our home—but not to that extent.

When I turned fifteen, my father attempted suicide on my birthday. The trauma of that event left a lasting impression on me. I struggled with feelings of guilt and helplessness, questioning whether I could have prevented it. The aftermath of his attempt was a period of confusion and grief, both for me and my family.

A couple of years later, Mom and I were in the parking lot of an O'Charley's, and Shirley Caesar's version of "O for a Thousand Tongues" played on the cassette. I loved gospel music, but most of the time it was too chaotic and repetitive for Mom. (As a mom with anxiety myself, I get it now. Sorry, Mom.) But for some reason, that song that day hit Mom like a load of bricks, and she lost it. I had never seen her cry like that. This was sobbing, full-on ugly crying, and she told me she was thinking about leaving Dad.

I understood even then why she'd want to. Leave him, I mean. I lived with him, too. But I also wondered what would happen to him if she did. He wasn't a perfect dad, but he was mine. She didn't leave. She was faithful to her vow of, "'til death do us part," but I don't think she was happy. She was loyal. She was dutiful. When he was diagnosed with stage IV melanoma fifteen years later, she became his full-time caregiver. She carried on with stoic endurance. Watching her navigate those challenges with such resilience and duty was both inspiring and heartbreaking.

These experiences shaped my understanding of fear, anxiety, and loyalty. They taught me that our reactions to life's challenges are often rooted in the complexities of our past. As a mother now, I reflect on how they have influenced my approach to parenthood, relationships, and my understanding of mental health.

I've wondered whether my mother ever aspired to be more like her mother, despite their contrasting personalities. As my therapist noted in one of our sessions, I sometimes long to be more like my mom. She was a loyal and dutiful wife and a loyal and dutiful daughter. When Mamaw developed dementia shortly after my dad passed away, my mom began to care for her full-time.

My therapist stopped me when relaying this story and asked, "Is that who you think you are as well? The dutiful daughter?" It hit me like a load of bricks, and I completely lost it. I was reminded of the movie *Spanglish*. The mother, played by Paz Vega, comes to grips with the idea that her daughter wants a life different from her own, while the daughter discovers her identity rests on one fact: that she is her mother's daughter.

Mom and Mamaw shared a unique relationship, more akin to sisters than the traditional mother-daughter dynamic. Mamaw, who became a mother at seventeen and whose husband was a war veteran, was a vibrant and spiritual presence in our family. She lived out her role as a pastor's wife with charisma and devotion that left a lasting impression. I grew up hearing stories of Papaw's war experiences and his vow to dedicate his life to the ministry, a vow that shaped our family's life for generations.

Mamaw was the Spirit-filled social butterfly, hands lifted high in the second pew—the front pew was for men only. Her practical, introverted daughter observed all the goings-on from the back pew. Mamaw was a born pastor's wife, thriving in the limelight and effortlessly living up to everyone's ideals. Especially in later years, she was known as a mighty prayer warrior. She'd stop and pray for strangers in public and occasionally for the best parking space. (I swear to God, it opened up every time.) Coincidentally, Mom's caregiver at the facility, Maria, told me that Mom is "a prayer warrior." She seems to know when Maria is in pain and lays her hand on her shoulder and prays for her. I told Maria that Mom is just like her mother in that way. When I posted about this on Facebook, family members said she looked more and more like Mamaw every day.

I read a book recommended to me by a friend called *Signs*, written by Laura Lynn Jackson. It's about the idea that the universe will send you signs and messages to communicate with you and steer you to a higher path. I couldn't help but think about Mamaw's signature parking spot miracle. When magical coincidences happen, whether we regard them as miracles or random occurrences comes down to personal belief. The book even mentions praying for a parking space to open. I am always fascinated by these "huh" moments when I realize that an experience I had within the church parallels experiences outside of it as part of other belief systems. When you grow up being told your exact understanding of faith is the only truth, any outside perspective becomes threatening.

The book also provided some unexpected comfort. The author explained how our relationship with those who pass to the other side doesn't end. The person who passed actually has the capacity to love the ones left behind more fully and completely than they ever did while in human form.

One story is of a mother's adult son who committed suicide on her birthday. After connecting with the soul through signs, Laura Lynn came to understand the child, in his sickness, was seeking a way to be forever connected to his mother. This perspective helped me understand how or why Dad might have chosen my birthday to attempt his exit. He loved me, even if his sickness prevented him from expressing it in a healthy way. Even though he lived fifteen more years before passing from cancer, I could see, from the other side, that he loved me perfectly, and I could forgive and seek to love him and others more fully.

In the maze of family dynamics, we often find ourselves lost in complex emotions and experiences that shape our adult lives. My journey through fear, anxiety, and loyalty, rooted in my childhood and the emotionally absent relationship with my father, serves as a testament to this.

As a daughter who witnessed her mother's loyalty in the face of adversity, I learned early on about the weight of duty and the resilience it demands. Reflecting on these experiences, it becomes evident that our coping mechanisms and responses to life's challenges are often inherited from, or at least influenced by, our familial interactions.

LET'S CHECK IN

Consider how your own past, with its unique blend of experiences, has shaped your present. Understand that the fears and anxieties we carry often have deep roots in our childhood experiences and family dynamics. These experiences, though painful, also offer valuable lessons.

Reflect on how the ways you learned to cope as a child now influence your adult life. Are they serving you well, or is it time to reevaluate and learn healthier ways? Remember, our past doesn't have to dictate our future. We have the power to heal, grow, and choose different paths for ourselves. Even in the darkest moments, there is hope for recovery and renewal. Your journey, like mine, is one of continuous learning, healing, and transformation.

For you, dear reader, I invite you to delve into your own family history. Explore how the dynamics within your family have influenced your approach to life. Consider the following:

Identify inherited patterns: Reflect on the patterns and behaviors you've observed and possibly inherited from your family. How have these influenced your response to stress, relationships, and life choices?

Acknowledge emotional legacies: Understand that emotions like fear and anxiety can be unfortunate legacies passed down through generations. Recognizing this can help you address and heal these deep-seated emotions.

Seek therapy: I sound like a broken record here, but if family trauma continues to impact your life, consider seeking therapy.

Practice self-compassion: Be kind to yourself as you navigate these complex emotions. I have a tattoo on my wrist of a tiny arrow, reminding me that healing is indeed a direction in motion, not a destination. Be present with your emotions without over-identifying with them. Replace critical or negative thoughts about yourself with affirmations and positive statements. Remind yourself of your strengths, accomplishments, and the progress you've made.

Write your story: Like I did, you can redefine your narrative. Write your story, embracing both the challenges and triumphs. This can be a powerful tool for healing and transformation, as it has been for me.

In my case, the burden of duty and the scars of trauma became part of my identity. It was a role I was accustomed to playing. A good girl. A dutiful daughter. I was coming face-to-face with the reality that I was deeply flawed and human, capable of hurting others and myself. Maybe I was afraid that if my supportive community knew the reality, they wouldn't keep showing up for me. Or maybe I felt like if I acknowledged the truth, I didn't deserve their support. For me, unpacking experiences, more than anything else, was the genesis of finding self-compassion and freedom.

Crafting a family or personal history is a great way to unpack your past and reflect on its influence on you as an adult. Here are several guided questions you can consider exploring as journal prompts or for writing a memoir. Whether you share it with others is up to you.

Family roots and beginnings: What are the origins of your family? Consider ancestral homelands, immigration stories, or notable events that mark the beginning of your family's history.

Influential ancestors: Were there any ancestors or family members who played a significant role in shaping your family's story? What were their lives like, and how did they influence the family?

Cultural heritage: How has your family's cultural background influenced your upbringing and values? Include traditions, languages, religious practices, or customs that are significant to your family.

Family dynamics and relationships: What were/are the dynamics like within your family? Consider relationships between parents, siblings, and extended family, and how these dynamics have evolved over time.

Significant family events: Were there any significant events or periods that had a profound impact on your family? These could include wars, migrations, economic hardships, or memorable gatherings.

Challenges and triumphs: What major challenges has your family faced, and how were they overcome? Reflect on the resilience and strength your family showed during tough times.

Personal childhood memories: What are your earliest and most vivid memories of growing up in your family? How do these memories contribute to your understanding of your family's history?

Family's contribution and legacy: In what ways has your family contributed to the community or made a mark in history? This could be at a local, national, or even international level.

Remember, journaling or writing a memoir is not just about recounting facts but also about capturing the emotions, lessons, and spirit of your family's journey. You can use it as a tool for personal healing or document your experience for future generations.

4

Treating Mental Health as Physical Health

"Tell me, what is it you plan to do with your one wild and precious life?"

—Mary Oliver

It's funny how sometimes cleaning our physical spaces can help us clear our mental space too. I know I'm guilty of not being able to focus until my surroundings are tidy and organized. But let's be real, sometimes life throws bigger obstacles our way than just a messy desk. For me, that obstacle was financial instability. It's amazing how much that can consume your thoughts and infiltrate your everyday life.

Anxiety often isolates us, making us feel alone in our struggles. However, moments of genuine connection, like an unforgettable concert-going experience that I described in chapter two, remind us that we are part of something larger. Engaging in activities that bring you joy, whether it's music, art, or being in nature, can be a powerful antidote to anxiety. These experiences provide perspective, helping us to see beyond our immediate worries and connect with a deeper sense of purpose and belonging.

In his book, *Hardwiring Happiness*, Rick Hanson describes the brain as Velcro for negative experiences and Teflon for positive ones.[2] The brain is better at remembering painful events, but we can trick it into rewiring itself by focusing on positive experiences. Consider the activities, places, and experiences that bring you a sense of peace and connection. Think about how you can incorporate these elements into your daily life to create a refuge from the stresses of the world.

One of my chronic stressors is financial instability. So when that trigger is pulled, it can have disastrous results. I know from experience, as you'll soon read. But what I've learned is the universe has a way of correcting your path and leading you to a better outcome, if you'll allow it. This trigger was ultimately what led me to discover that I am a sanctuary.

The following stories are my personal experiences in which I learned the importance of having a support system around me, the challenges of juggling family and financial responsibilities, and the constant search for contentment and stability.

---

[2] Rick Hanson, *Hardwiring Happiness: The New Brain Science of Contentment, Calm, and Confidence* (New York: Random House, 2013), 27.

When we moved from Orlando in 2012, we signed a two-year lease on a rental in East Nashville. It was an adorable bungalow in a great location, but with only 1,400 square feet and two kids, we quickly felt the lack of space. My husband, Nathan, kept looking at listings online and telling me about how the prices were really rising in this area. I said I'd start looking just to keep tabs on the market in the event we wanted to buy when our lease was up.

I drove by a few listings to compare what they looked like online to in person. I turned the corner and entered one of the most beautiful streets I've ever seen—Heatherbrook. It was October, and vibrant yellow, red, and brown leaves peppered the air and the ground. Streams of light pierced through tall cedar and oak trees that soared over the paved street. It was serene, quaint, and almost otherworldly. And then I saw it. I took one look at this house and knew it was going to be our next home, our "forever" home. I couldn't shake the feeling. I felt an inexplicable sense that we belonged to each other.

After snapping back into reality, I called Nathan at work and said, "I just found our house." I shot an email off to our landlord to test the waters and see if it would be at all feasible.

She said, "I think we can work something out," and that she supported anyone who wanted to invest in East Nashville. This community spirit echoed throughout our time there, and we knew we had found a special place. The sellers accepted our offer, and I couldn't believe it was happening so smoothly and quickly.

Then, in December 2012, two weeks after we moved, I lost my job. I received a phone call that said the company where I had worked for the past five years had been sold. I began seeking out freelance jobs. Emmeline wasn't even six months old, and I had to balance her full-time care with the need to make a full-time income.

There were stretches when I had regular income and others when I didn't. Since I didn't have a job, I decided to get involved at Rowan's school by helping to raise money for the PTO (parent-teacher organization). Rallying community members to participate in fundraisers and collecting donations for school projects felt immensely rewarding and gave me something to do with the baby at my side. I turned my sights to the larger community and started advocating for locally zoned schools. I helped organize tailgating at the high school football games, and I found countless opportunities to connect with community members and share stories about the importance of getting involved. Responding to need brought out a new dimension of life that made all this even more meaningful. I remember feeling more alive and fulfilled than I ever had. The truth is the community support was already there; I simply found a place to plug in and contribute.

We made a lot of wonderful memories in our home and community over the next two and a half years. During the warmer months, I made it a tradition to shop yard sales in the neighborhood with the girls. Almost always someone would offer Rowan something for free. At one of these sales, Rowan found an *ochoko* or sake cup, with the word "Lucky" written on it in both Japanese and English.

Rowan had long had an interest in Eastern culture, from TV shows to attending Chinese camp to practicing Karate for three years. This cup would become her favorite—she called it her "lucky cup"—and it fit her perfectly. Just like the house and neighborhood fit our family. We were indeed lucky.

But a financial storm began to brew from the aftermath of losing full-time work two years earlier and having a toddler at home. By 2015, we had no savings, and our credit cards were maxed out. Panic set in. Although I didn't realize it at the time, that's when I began to experience major anxiety. By the summer, we didn't have money for extra expenses, like fixing our brakes, or the AC that had gone out in our family car, or our broken freezer. There was a woeful lack of ice cream in our lives. We also didn't have enough money to travel to Florida to see our family (or go anywhere for that matter). That also meant we had to pull out of a friend's wedding in which the kids had been asked to participate. As a chronic people pleaser, I absolutely hated letting our friends down. It was tough to deliver that news, and I realized that a lot of other people had it much, much worse. We were privileged. Our situation was not dire. We just weren't making enough to support our lifestyle. I felt I had to do something to reverse the tide.

Knowing how much the value of homes had risen in the area, I realized that by selling our beloved house, we could alleviate our financial discomfort, pay off our credit cards, and start fresh. Nathan was agreeable, so we did. I desperately wanted to stay in the neighborhood where we had spent the last three years planting roots, building friendships, and working in the community. To do that, we bought a little house that was considerably smaller and older (built in 1949) and only two miles away. I called it "the little green house." It was at the top of our budget. Still, we were lucky. It had tons of character and a great big fenced-in backyard. Best of all, we hit the "neighbor jackpot." We met some dear friends on the adjacent streets to the house who also had kids at our school. They invited us into their village to do life together, and I had no idea how much I would become utterly dependent upon their support in just a few years.

At the same time as the move, my longtime friend started a company and asked me to work for him. It was part-time work, but he believed it wouldn't be long until it transitioned into full-time work. It provided a steady income and allowed me to work from home. But adjusting to a smaller house (again) was difficult.

Over the next two years living in the little green house, Nathan and I had ongoing conversations about how to make the house work for us. We were grateful to be recovering financially and making better decisions. We didn't want to keep accruing debt by adding on or building out. It was a constant exercise in learning to be content, especially when we were battling a brown recluse infestation that we spent hundreds of dollars to control (*shudder*). Every time we climbed into bed or put shoes on, we each had to do a spider check. I remember seeing Emmeline sit on the floor when a brown recluse climbed out of the pile of toys from the basket next to her.

Around this same time, Mom had begun showing symptoms of memory loss, and this terrified me. At the urging of my brother, I began making monthly trips to monitor her progress and make sure her needs were taken care of. I always brought the kids. On one of these trips, while I was driving, I felt a shooting pain through the right side of my chest that felt like I was being stabbed. I knew since it wasn't the left side, I was likely experiencing panic and not a heart attack. But I also feared that I might have neuropathy, which I thought could indicate diabetes or cancer.

Anxiety looks for a means of expression or meaning to which it attaches. It needs a host, like a parasite. It was too difficult for me to identify the emotional stressors weighing on me; it felt easier to identify a physical ailment. In secret, I bought blood sugar testing strips and A1C tests and took them. I had to know, before I went to the doctor, what I was dealing with. The tests were negative, and the doctor literally laughed when I explained my symptoms and self diagnosis. He told me what I was experiencing was * a n x i e t y *.

This was a relief—I didn't have cancer. But would awareness be enough to alleviate my symptoms? (Side note, I promptly switched primary care providers to someone professional and caring enough to not laugh in my face.) I would come to need more professional help, and thankfully, I fell into the care of a great therapist.

In therapy, I discovered that anxiety often thrives in the shadows of unaddressed emotional needs and unspoken fears. It feeds on the silence around our deepest struggles, growing more potent in the void of neglect. As I navigated through the sessions, the layers of my anxiety began to unfold, revealing the underlying emotional stressors that had long been ignored or minimized.

Let this be a reminder that anxiety is not just a condition to be silenced but a signal to be understood. It often points to deeper emotional needs and unresolved conflicts within us. Just as I learned to confront and understand my anxiety, you too can embark on this journey of self-discovery. Therapy can be a great tool, not just for alleviating symptoms but for understanding the self.

The first time I stepped into my counselor's office, my face was numb. I had just come from having a root canal (caused by chronic teeth clenching from stress). I was a mess, physically and emotionally. Minutes into the session, I began to cry and couldn't stop. The release came when I knew I was in a place I could unload. I rarely gave my therapist space to speak about my situation. It took months for me to slow down and allow her to make connections and speak her wisdom. She once told me that I came in as if I was "holding stories," just waiting to get them out. That felt true. The practice of telling them, in itself, was therapeutic.

Most of my "stories" were about the people in my care around me. I would check out when she'd turn it back to me, asking, "What do you think you need?" I responded with a blank stare and silence.

But slowly, I was learning. I began coming to terms with my anxiety and began doing a lot of emotional work. I even told a friend, "I have learned so much about myself In the past two years. I feel like

I'm a different person. If I had known what I know now, I think I would have handled things differently two years ago." I realized that my anxiety blinded me from believing I had options. I did what I thought was best at the time (selling the house), but I still dealt with major regret (what if we had waited a bit longer?).

I also realized the changes forced me to deal with my anxiety head-on. I'm grateful for that. My kids often asked us, "Why did we move?" Little Emmeline would refer to the old house as the "sunny house." It was painful knowing the instability I felt like I had created. But I was glad that at least Rowan was able to stay in the same elementary school. And they both had lots of neighbor friends to play with.

Then, in the late summer of 2017, Nathan got the itch to move. Nearly two years to the day that we'd moved in, he began talking to me about moving (again) so we'd have more space. He pointed out how anxious I had been since we moved. He was right. I knew the house would not be a long-term fit for us, but the timing seemed awful. Terrible, in fact. It was the end of summer break, and school was about to start back. Emmeline was going into kindergarten! I had just started working full-time, and I knew a move would be an enormous time-suck.

I reluctantly began to declutter and pack and look for houses. We wanted to stay in the area; after all, Nathan still worked at the neighborhood middle school. Rowan was now going there, too. But I knew this time we probably wouldn't be able to stay close by.

Honestly, I was crushed. It seemed inevitable we would end up with different schools for the kids.

We found one house we liked in a suburb in a different part of town, but we couldn't get an offer on it fast enough. Then we were able to put an offer on another house but were outbid. Finally, we found a third house somewhat nearby and had an offer accepted. Still, I was grieving. I went back to counseling after taking a break over the summer, and I began prepping the kids for the move as I packed the house. We kept playing up the benefits of the move, and we kept telling ourselves that this was it. We wouldn't be moving again for a long time. We were grateful the new house would still be close enough to maintain some of our existing connections, but I also knew we'd have to completely rebuild our social life in the new area. New schools, new friends—all of it.

A couple of weeks later at the grocery store, I ran into a neighbor from our "sunny house" on Heatherbrook. He told me the people who had bought our old place had moved out and were going to sell it. My heart started racing ... What were the chances? I threw a couple of things in my cart and checked out. My head was spinning. We were under contract with the other house, so what could we do? It seemed crazy to even think about it.

I kind of sheepishly asked Nathan if we should message the owner of our old house—just to see what she was planning to sell it for. He said, "Give it a shot."

I wrote her a message on Facebook but felt so embarrassed that I deleted it—I mean, what a crazy idea, right? Who does this? But she had already seen it, and she responded later that night. They too had moved back into their old house. But they had not made any concrete plans to sell the sunny house just yet. They were considering making it an Airbnb. But if we were interested, she said she could tell us about the half-plans she'd made so far. My real estate agent knew her, so he called and talked to her as well. She told him for some reason the house just never really felt like it was theirs, and they even referred to the house as ours.

The next morning, she decided she was willing to sell it back to us. Nathan and the girls were in the room when our realtor told us over speakerphone. In that moment, the floodgates opened, and I began hardcore ugly crying. The kids were jumping up and down screaming with delight. I cried off and on for hours—I was feeling waves of relief and joy. I could not believe it. We were getting our old house back!

I was in awe, really. I thought back to the chain of events that brought us to this place. There is no way we could have ever orchestrated it. What if I hadn't seen the neighbor in the grocery store? What if I pushed back on Nathan when he wanted to sell? What if someone different had bought the house when we sold it? What if we weren't able to cancel our contract on the other house? My therapist applauded me for having the courage to ask for what I wanted. I then realized why it felt so vulnerable and awkward to ask in the first place. I didn't believe I should have needs. I was more comfortable feeling emotional when my needs weren't met than asking someone to meet me there and risk having them say no.

Although my religious faith had taken a deep dive in recent years, I had no other explanation than the mystical, miraculous nature of the universe to thank for this series of events. Even the seller called it a "God thing." We talked about how strange and wonderful it is to have a sense of place, a sanctuary. It felt like such a gift. And we were overjoyed to be home. The seller (who is a real estate agent herself) texted me the day we moved back in about Rowan's lucky cup: "You left the lucky cup at the house when we moved in. Since then, it has been in several of my listings for luck. I happened to have it in my car today and left it for you. I truly believe it is lucky."

Getting our house back felt like the greatest gift. It felt like redemption in a physical form. Still, in all my striving for contentment when I lived in "exile" at the little green house, I wondered what it was about the house that was so special to me. Material things are just that—material. What about the house represented a longing in me, beneath the surface?

I had been chewing on those thoughts for a while when a songwriter, Ryan O'Neal, known by the band name Sleeping At Last, released a collection of songs inspired by the Enneagram. I listened intently when "Six" was released.

> *I had the most vivid dream*
> *My feet had left the ground*

I was floating to heaven

But I could only look down

My mind was heavy

Running ragged with worst-case scenarios

Emergency exits and the distance below

I woke up so worried that the angels let go

Oh, God, I'm so tired

Of being afraid

What would it feel like

To put this baggage down?

If I'm being honest

I'm not sure I'd know how

I want to take shelter, but I'm ready, ready to fight

Somewhere in the middle, I feel a little paralyzed

Maybe I'm stronger

Than I realize

I want to believe

No, I choose to believe

That I was made to become

A sanctuary

Fear won't go away

But I can keep it at bay

These invisible walls

Just might keep us safe
With a vigilant heart
I'll push into the dark
And I'll learn to breathe deep
And make peace with the stars
Is it courage or faith
To show up every day?
To trust that there will be light
Always waiting behind
Even the darkest of nights
No matter what
Somehow we'll be okay
Don't be afraid [3]

I wept while listening to the song. The word "sanctuary" fastened itself to my heart, and I knew in an instant what the house was meant to show me: I am the sanctuary.

My beloved house represented all the things that I was made to offer myself and others in my care: safety, shelter, a place to belong, and protection from the outside elements. I had been content to be a doormat when, in fact, I was the sanctuary.

---

[3] Sleeping At Last, "Six," track 6 on *Atlas: Enneagram*, self-released, 2019, digital. Lyrics used with permission.

My journey, fraught with anxiety and uncertainty, taught me that embracing change and trusting my intuition are crucial. Anxiety often blinds us, making us believe we are devoid of options. Yet, the path to finding our sanctuary lies in recognizing our inner strength and the choices we have, even in the bleakest of times.

As you navigate through your own challenges, remember that change is not only inevitable but necessary for growth. Trusting your intuition, embracing change, and confronting anxiety can lead you to discover your inner sanctuary. This realization is empowering—it reminds us that we are more resilient and capable than we often give ourselves credit for. The journey to finding your sanctuary may be long and winding, but it is a path worth taking, filled with lessons, growth, and ultimately, a deeper understanding of self.

LET'S CHECK IN

The concept of sanctuary, more than just a physical space, is a metaphor for the peace and strength we hold within ourselves. As you reflect on your journey, consider the role of your inner sanctuary.

Intuition as your door: Your intuition is your inner wisdom. By tuning in to your intuition, you align your actions with your deepest values and truths. This inner guidance helps you navigate challenges and make decisions that resonate with your true self.

Self-acceptance as a foundation: Embracing yourself as you are is the cornerstone of your personal sanctuary. Self-acceptance allows you to acknowledge both your strengths and vulnerabilities without judgment. This acceptance creates a space of peace and self-love, enabling you to grow and evolve while staying true to yourself.

Boundaries as protective walls: Just as a sanctuary has boundaries that protect its sacred space, setting personal boundaries safeguards your emotional and mental well-being. These boundaries help you define where you end and others begin, allowing you to interact with the world without losing your sense of self. They serve as a reminder of your priorities and values, keeping you aligned with what truly matters to you.

Gratitude as light: Practicing gratitude transforms your inner sanctuary into a space of abundance. Gratitude shifts your focus away from what you lack and onto appreciating what you have.

Remember, your inner sanctuary is a sacred space where you can retreat, recharge, and realign with your true self. With these practices, you strengthen your sanctuary, ensuring it remains a source of peace, strength, and guidance.

Creating a physical sanctuary in your home is a wonderful way to foster a sense of peace, safety, and relaxation. Here are some tips:

Choose the right space: Identify a spot in your home where you feel most at ease. It could be a small corner, a closet, or even a whole room if you have the space. The key is to choose a place that feels separate from the areas associated with stress or work.

Make it comfortable: Add cushions, a cozy chair, a soft rug, or one of those cool egg chairs. Ensure that the seating is comfortable enough for you to relax for extended periods. Invest in a luxury robe you feel good and pampered in to wear when you're visiting your sanctuary.

Control the lighting: Natural light can be uplifting, but if your sanctuary is indoors, consider soft, warm lighting. You might use candles, fairy lights, or a lamp with a dimmer to create a calming ambiance.

Incorporate nature: If possible, include elements of nature, such as plants, crystals, or even a view of your yard.

Minimize distractions: Ensure your sanctuary is a tech-free zone, or at least limit electronic devices.

Personalize your space: Decorate your sanctuary with items that have personal significance and make you feel calm and at peace. This could be photos, artwork, meaningful quotes, or memorabilia that make you feel good.

Add soothing sounds: Consider the role of sound in your sanctuary. Gentle music, nature sounds, or the soothing hum of a small water feature can enhance relaxation.

Include aromatherapy: Scents can have a powerful effect on mood. Use essential oils, scented candles, or incense to create a calming atmosphere. Lavender, chamomile, and sandalwood are great options for relaxation.

Create a ritual: If you're task-oriented like me, you'll need a routine or ritual that you perform in your sanctuary. It could be morning meditation, evening journaling, or a simple stretching routine. This ritual will reinforce the sanctuary's purpose and help you transition into a relaxed state.

Remember, the goal is to create a space that resonates with your personal idea of peace and tranquility. This sanctuary is your personal haven, a place where you can recharge, reflect, and find calm. You not only deserve this, dear friend, you need it.

5

Dealing with Life's Curveballs

"We are all walking repositories of buried treasure."

— **Elizabeth Gilbert**

It's a feeling that hits you like a ton of bricks—that moment when you realize nothing will ever be the same. Maybe it comes after a phone call or a diagnosis that you never saw coming. Suddenly, your world is tilting on its axis, and you're left wondering how to pick up the pieces.

As someone who has been there, I know how hard it can be. There are days when it feels like you're barely holding on, when the weight of grief and fear can take your breath. It's in those moments that what truly matters becomes crystal clear: your relationships and the memories you want to make.

In this chapter, I share the tough reality of those moments of change for our family in hopes anyone who has been in a similar situation can identify with the weight of grief and fear and find some comfort from knowing that this, too, shall pass. Life will never be the same, but it's still good.

In the summer of 2019, Nathan began to experience strange symptoms. He had a loss of energy, felt depressed, and soon began to develop weakness and numbness on his left side. We thought it was a side effect of a new blood pressure medication he was taking, which he stopped immediately. His doctor began to run tests and kept a careful watch because they couldn't find a pulse in his foot. During the next three weeks, the numbness and weakness in his foot gradually spread up his leg to his arm, hand, and face. He said it felt like he had an extra layer of skin. He had developed a limp, too.

Monday morning, August 26, 2019, Nathan was already at work when he sent an email to his doctor describing weakness and numbness on his left side. The day before, he had reached into his bag for his EarPods and couldn't feel what he was touching. He knew something was really wrong, but we still thought it was a neurological side effect of the medication. He emailed her out of an abundance of caution. She emailed him back and told him to go to the ER immediately. By 9:30 a.m., Nathan was at the hospital, and they took him straight back for diagnostics. By 10:00, I had arrived. I situated myself in the corner chair with my laptop open, ready to continue working and intercept emails as they came in from clients. Nathan lay in the bed with his gray slacks, black polo shirt, and dress shoes. I remember thinking it was strange to see him in his work clothes in this hospital setting. Everything felt surreal. Minutes later, an ER doctor came in and said the results of the CT scan showed an "abnormality." The word seemed to materialize in the air. With it, my hand reached up to the top of my laptop and slowly lowered it shut.

They ordered an MRI and a second CT scan. A couple of hours later, a neurosurgeon came in and started explaining a little more, using words like "tumor" and "cancer." I began to dissociate. It all felt too surreal, as if we were hearing them talk about someone else. Not Nathan. And surely these were all worst-case scenarios and not what we were actually facing. We waited in the busy ER for more answers and to be admitted. I thought whatever was in there, they would surely be in a rush to cut out, and then we would be on the other side of this awful, terrible news.

The next day, Tuesday, August 27, 2019, was day two in the ER. Vanderbilt was such a busy hospital they had no beds on the neurology floor, so we were staying in a room in the ER. Our friend Julie had been taking care of our kids, and she brought them to see us so we could tell them in person what the doctors found. This would become the second worst moment of my life. Nathan kept it as upbeat and hopeful as possible by cracking jokes and blowing up latex gloves like balloons, and I laid the news on them, "Daddy has a brain tumor. The doctors are going to take care of it, and he is going to be okay."

I have no idea how they felt or what they were experiencing because they didn't have a big emotional reaction. My heart was breaking for them, and they were probably feeling confused and anxious. Maintaining a sense of normalcy seemed important, so I asked Julie to take them to school. At this point, we were still thinking there was a possibility of surgery that day or the next.

Finally, we were taken to a room in neurology, and Dr. Whitman came in to discuss the results. She kept her bag draped across her body, and she remained very tense and matter-of-fact. She was there to explain more about the tumor. She started by saying there was a 1 percent chance that it was not a tumor but some sort of abscess, which would have been preferred, obviously. But most likely, it was a tumor.

There are two types of tumors: primary and metastatic. The second CT scan of his body showed no visible tumors anywhere else, so we knew we were looking at a primary tumor in the brain. She added that metastatic tumors respond well to radiation. Primary tumors are a little tougher. The tumor was about three centimeters round and located in the right side of the brain above the motor strip. Because of its location, it was considered high risk, and she said she would not do surgery because of the risk of paralyzation. Even if they did remove the tumor, they can never guarantee 100 percent removal, she told us, and patients still have to undergo radiation and chemotherapy. She said that, most likely, the course of action (also known as standard of care) would be radiation and chemo. But she reiterated we'd know more once the pathology results came back.

My mind reeled with these bleak realities, and I felt my stomach turning. I knew I was close to losing my composure, and I didn't want to cry in front of Nathan at such an intense moment. Dr. Whitman asked if we had any questions, and the hopelessness in the room was so palpable that neither of us could manage a single one. The air hung hot and thick on the yellowed hospital room walls. I excused myself and walked out of the room as my eyes welled up. As soon as I was out of earshot around the corner, I burst out crying, leaning into the wall. I slowly slid down and crumpled over into a little ball on the floor, my head in my lap, flooding my hands with hot, wet tears and snot. I don't ever remember feeling more intense fear and hopelessness. We had not been given a single sliver of hope or good news. We had been given a death sentence.

I called Julie on my cell and relayed as much of the new information as I could, and she did her best to console me. This was the worst-case scenario, and she felt the weight of it along with me. After we hung up, a hospital worker came over. She spoke with an accent indicating she was from the islands, and a spirit of comfort abounded. She said, "Is that your husband in there? Oh goodness, he's going to be just fine. Honey, God's got this! You don't have to worry." I wondered if she was right. Since he was so young and healthy, surely he had a better chance of a positive outcome.

Navigating the complexities of Nathan's diagnosis felt like walking a tightrope. It was a delicate balance of being a support pillar while grappling with my own fears and uncertainties. The challenge was not only to support him but to maintain a semblance of normalcy for our children, who would be equally affected by the seismic shift in our family.

In those moments, as we returned to the semblance of our daily life, I found myself constantly oscillating between being a caregiver and a partner, a mother and an individual grappling with her own emotions. The burden of the diagnosis was not mine, yet it loomed over every thought and action.

Thistle Farms is a Nashville-based nonprofit for women survivors of trafficking, prostitution, and addiction. They have a for-profit arm that employs these survivors to create self-care products and gifts, and they have a local cafe. My friend Margaux has worked for the organization for years. Her husband became one of my husband's best friends, so when we faced our biggest challenge to date, she was one of the first people I talked to. She told me that at Thistle Farms, they have a saying for moments like these: trouble and joy, sickness and wellness, anxiety and peace: Everybody gets a turn.

"Congratulations, it's your turn," she said.

As we progressed through Nathan's treatment, the importance of community became more evident. Our friends, neighbors, and extended family provided not only emotional support but practical help that was invaluable. This experience underscored the importance of building and nurturing a support network. In times of crisis, these relationships become a lifeline.

We knew we would never be the same after this. How could we be? One of my best friends texted me the week of the biopsy as I was processing the news and the grief and said, "Lean into it. Life will never be the same, better or worse, but it's still good."

People would kindly ask me, "But how are YOU doing?" I told my friend Stella, who survived breast cancer, that for me, now felt like the easy part. The energy was climactic, and we had all this support and attention. I knew that in the weeks and months to come my involvement would increase and get more difficult to manage. I had been swept up into an inciting incident—a story I had no choice but to participate in. Playing a supporting role and having things to do gave me a sense of agency and purpose.

The first couple of weeks, I had very little mental clarity and found that I had to concentrate to do simple tasks. I remember when I left the hospital for the first time post-diagnosis. I had to concentrate so hard on operating the car, finding the exit to the parking garage, remembering what roads to take, and how fast or slow to drive. It was like I was peering through a fog.

I also had very little emotional regulation. I cried often at the drop of a hat, especially when I was alone. Other days, I could barely summon any emotion at all. One day, a close friend dropped off homemade bread and flowers, and she broke down. I smiled and stared at her, feeling completely numb and unable to cry. I imagine both responses were normal in a situation like this. My paranoia kicked up, too. I felt like my health was at risk, or something was going to happen to me, too, which only fueled the fear and the panic. Nighttime was usually worse. My chronic heart palpitations increased, and I had nightmares that I was having to take chemo.

I was swimming in grief. Or more like doggy-paddling. I didn't have time or money to continue therapy during this season. I had put sessions on pause. I was missing school activities we did every year with the kids, like Walk to School Day, and getting long-distance updates about Mom's declining mental state. I felt I had no one I could talk to about how I was feeling, like I used to with my mom.

Hearing others talk about their normal life felt surreal, as if I was looking through a window. One night, I heard someone talking about some future vacation plans, and it reminded me that our lives, at least how we used to understand them, were on hold for the foreseeable future. There was no planning for our next vacation or house project. Our sole focus was cancer treatment and, hopefully, recovery.

Exactly one month after being diagnosed with an inoperable cancerous brain tumor, our little family packed up and drove to St. Louis, where Nathan would be admitted for surgery. It turned out there is no such thing as an inoperable brain tumor, just doctors unwilling to take the risks involved. After burning CDs of scans and FedExing them to several doctors for second, third, and fourth opinions, the consensus from doctors in New York to New Mexico was that there was a clear clinical benefit to resecting the tumor—essentially removing the bulk of it since they can't cut out the entire thing—before we started radiation and possibly chemo.

Something that comes with the territory of having a brain tumor is that surgeons can't cut a margin around the tumor. Glioblastomas have little finger-like tentacles that infiltrate the brain tissue. So once his incision was healed, Nathan started six weeks of radiation designed to target a margin around the resection.

There's nothing like facing the world's most lethal and aggressive cancer to cause you to take inventory of your life, your values, and your relationships. (Easy for me to say because I wasn't the one with the tumor.) And yet at some point, each of us will face a similar burden. We all get a turn, as my friend said. One of the words that kept coming up for me was alignment. Choosing behaviors that are consistent with our values brings an enormous amount of peace. So does learning to surrender our false sense of security and control. Forgiveness is another. Those were not fighting postures. One friend said most people spend their entire lives running from death (and consequently making horrible decisions).

In Don Miller's podcast, *Building a StoryBrand*, he interviewed Rebekah Lyons, who wrote a book called *Rhythms of Renewal*. In it, she talks about the physical effects of stress and anxiety. She told Don:

> "I think forgiveness really is a gateway to healing for so many of us. We don't realize how crippling resentment or bitterness can become, how it can become literally a tumor. It can be something physically our bodies can't even hold on to."[4]

I am not insinuating that this tumor grew from that place. The doctors have told us Glioblastomas happen randomly. They don't have hereditary or environmental causes that Nathan would have been exposed to. I'm simply saying this physical journey caused us to turn inward, and the emotional journey helped us deal with matters all too easily shoved to the back of our day-to-day lives. When a reminder of your mortality gets shoved in your face, life has a way of prioritizing itself. We are emotional, irrational creatures. Surrender from control, rest from productivity, forgiveness, and release of pain are not our natural tendencies. But they open the gates of healing and freedom.

---

[4] Donald Miller, "Rebekah Lyons—The Magic of 'Less' to Manage Stress," 2019, in *Business Made Simple with Donald Miller*, produced by Donald Miller Words, podcast, mp3, 53:56, https://podcasts.apple.com/us/podcast/rebekah-lyons-the-magic-of-less-to-manage-stress/id1092751338?i=1000452614311.

When Nathan was diagnosed, I read this book called *When Life Gives You Pears*, written by Jeannie Gaffigan about her journey of being diagnosed with a brain tumor. In our desperation for answers, I reached out to the doctor she named in the book as her doctor. We flew to NYC to meet with him and his staff and discussed Nathan's case. This doctor pioneered the use of a fluorescent purple dye that lights up the areas of the tumor during surgery. Though he pioneered the technique, it was used by all neurosurgeons, so it wasn't necessary for him to do the surgery for that specific reason. Ultimately, we decided on St. Louis because that surgeon would allow Nathan to be awake during surgery. Plus it was closer to home, less expensive, and more manageable for travel.

In the book, there was a quote that really resonated with me during this time: "'Tumorgate' turned out to be the catalyst for the radical revolution I desperately needed to reconstruct my priorities."[5] Her book, although hilarious and entertaining, centered on how her prognosis strengthened her faith in God, deepened her love for family and friends, and renewed her hope in humanity. I hoped the same for us.

Two doctors dated the formation of this tumor around the end of May. Coincidentally, that was when Nathan was let go from his job, which was easily the most stressful event of his adult life. He wrote a letter of forgiveness about that event and sent it to his boss. I know

---

[5] Jeannie Gaffigan, *When Life Gives You Pears: The Healing Power of Family, Faith, and Funny People.* (New York: Grand Central Publishing, 2019), 1.

he continued to work through that forgiveness each day as he took responsibility for his health and emotions, doing what he could to live in alignment with his values and be at peace.

As an Enneagram Three, Nathan's core fear was that he would be found to be a fraud—that deep down, he would be seen as worthless. Nothing could have been further from the truth. Fighting this shame would be a lifelong challenge for him. When he lost his job (in his mind, his ability to earn his value/worth), it opened a childhood wound that left him laid bare and exposed.

The summer prior, as a family, we watched *The Greatest Showman* featuring Hugh Jackman. We loved the story and the music, which reminded me of songs you'd hear in a Pentecostal church. Nathan had an especially strong emotional reaction to the Bearded Lady's character and her song, "This Is Me." The song deals with overcoming shame and stepping into the glory of self—not the false ego self, but the true diamond that you are. This is the core truth for an Enneagram Three, and it always delighted me to hear and see Nathan dancing and singing to this song when doing chores around and outside the house or pounding the steering wheel along to its beat.

We all have our battles with self-doubt and fear of inadequacy. His journey towards healing and self-acceptance illustrates that embracing our true selves, with all our flaws and strengths, is a path to personal peace. It's also a way to shine in our most authentic light. In this light, we find the truest expression of ourselves, free from the shadows of doubt and the weight of external expectations.

This chapter in our lives, while fraught with fear and uncertainty, was also a journey of discovery. It's a journey that many of you might be on or may face in the future. In these times, I urge you to hold onto hope, to reach out for support, and to embrace the lessons that such trials inevitably bring. It's in these moments that we often discover the true depth of our strength and the indomitable spirit of human resilience. Author, speaker, and counselor Chip Dodd calls it a buoyancy for life.[6]

It turns out loving your spouse is easier in sickness than in health. I did not expect this. I did things for my husband that previously I had only ever done for my babies: fed him, trimmed his nails, rubbed his feet, put lotion on him, read out loud to him, helped him go to the bathroom, and eventually changed his diapers. And as I sat rubbing his feet after hours in rehab one night, I thought about how effortless it felt to serve him. It was as if compassion reoriented my heart toward the one I should have willingly served all along.

When he was healthy, my love came with conditions. I was leaning into a deeper, more selfless version of love—one that I would have never experienced if not for a chance to be with him now. And Nathan received that love and boomeranged it right back to me, with hugs and kisses and countless times telling me, "thank you" and "you're so amazing." The PT and OT staff at the rehab institute

---

[6] Chip Dodd, lecture, Nashville, TN, date unknown, quoted by Cara Davis, https://www.chipdodd.com/.

praised the way we worked together as a team. One of them kept asking me, "Are you sure you're not a therapist?" because of my intuition in helping him maneuver. I loved the flattery. We were not made for sickness, but what grace we found in the midst of it.

To the degree that I was killing it as a supportive wife during my husband's toughest hour, inside I was crumbling with anxiety and depression. I was doing my best to help out with Mom, who was still living at home in East Tennessee, while experiencing the trauma and chaos of the aftermath of diagnosis and treatment.

At some point, I jotted down in my iPhone notes:

> i drove 978 miles last week
> averaged 3 hr 42 min sleep
> with pneumonia

It read like a very sad, incorrectly written haiku. During the mounting stress, I came down with pneumonia and bronchitis, which would span nine weeks. I bought masks to protect others in the hospitals. (This was just four months before COVID would break out, and there would be a run on masks. I had plenty.) I didn't have the option to slow down. Neither did Nathan.

As the reality of Nathan's diagnosis sunk in, our world turned into a whirlwind of doctor visits, alternative therapies, and financial calculations. The fear of financial ruin loomed large, a trigger that sent me spiraling into tears. Nathan's resolve, in contrast, seemed to grow stronger with each challenge. He was ready to fight at any cost, a determination that both inspired and frightened me.

The surgery was a turning point. Nathan, always the fighter, chose to pursue the most aggressive treatment option, even if it meant the possibility of paralysis. It was a decision that was as brave as it was terrifying. As his wife, I supported him wholeheartedly, yet I couldn't shake the fear of what our future might hold. The possibility of caring for a paralyzed husband was daunting. I longed for Nathan to acknowledge the weight of this reality that we both were facing.

On the day of the surgery, Nathan's brother, sister, her husband, our honorary "uncle" Johnny, the kids, and I planted ourselves in the waiting room, preparing for a long day of surgery. Stella stopped by with fancy donuts, and Johnny took turns taking the kids to the gift shop. While we sat there all day, a malfunction with their alarm system caused the lights and alarm to blare at regular intervals, mirroring our nerves that were on the brink.

After several hours, Dr. Mitchell took me aside to a briefing cubby in the waiting room. He said the surgery was a success—in that ninety-nine percent of the tumor was removed. He said they worked well together during the awake craniotomy. He said he was about to wrap up when he saw some residual tumor among the motor strip chords—the riskiest part to resect. He asked Nathan if he wanted to go after it, and he said yes. The doctor said because of that, Nathan had some "weakness" on his left side. I knew from surgery prep that "weakness" meant it would be hard for him to move. He said Nathan would likely go from the hospital to a rehabilitation center. He added that with therapy and time, that would improve. I thanked him, and he was off. I walked back into the waiting room with the faces of Nathan's loved ones staring at me, waiting for the report, and the tears started flowing. I relayed what the doctor told me. The doctor called the surgery "successful" and his paralysis "weakness," but it didn't at all feel like we were out of the woods. We didn't yet know the full severity of the outcome of the surgery—and how it would affect us all.

I did my best to keep everyone updated on social media with the most positive news. In private, I researched more about the disease and its prognosis. It was important to Nathan that our friends and family saw him as a fighter, a man brimming with resilience and determination. This portrayal wasn't false, but it was incomplete. It was a narrative that omitted the darker, more challenging aspects of our journey—the sleepless nights, the physical and emotional exhaustion, and the deep-seated fears about the future.

A friend whose employee's husband had the same cancer shared a Facebook group for wives of husbands with Glioblastoma. I read through the posts with morbid curiosity. I was desperate to know how long we'd have to do this, whatever this was, and what was coming down the road. It was the only outlet where people talked about the reality of this disease—that it's terminal. In my actual life, everyone talked about healing, getting past it, and living a long time, especially Nathan. And I would never say anything to the contrary. Hope was the only thing we had. But Nathan's quality of life, and mine as well, had taken a dive. I couldn't imagine the shell of a person I'd be if, in five, seven, or ten years, I was still a full-time caregiver to a paralyzed man with a compromised brain.

I immersed myself in research about Glioblastoma. The Facebook group became my sanctuary of truth. Here, I could confront the grim prognosis and share in the collective sorrow and understanding of others who walked a similar path. This group was a stark contrast to the world outside, where the dialogue was dominated by talk of healing and recovery. While such optimism was essential, it sometimes felt like a veneer over our painful reality. One study I read said the average outcome (life expectancy) post-diagnosis for a tumor that matched Nathan's pathology was seven months. I thought surely we'd get at least two more years. He was young and healthy and seemed so determined to beat this thing, but I underestimated this monster's power.

A couple of weeks after the surgery, Nathan was released from the inpatient rehab center to come home. He was still not walking. I never dreamed Nathan wouldn't walk out of the hospital after surgery, much less not come home. I certainly didn't think after weeks of rehab, he would still be wheelchair-bound.

When it became apparent Nathan would have a much steeper hill to climb to regain mobility, I texted friends with a wish list of hacks to make the house wheelchair accessible. Friends came and installed a ramp to the front door and railings in the bathroom and shower.

They did yard maintenance and decorated the porches for fall to welcome us home. A good friend of ours organized a GoFundMe, and my fears of financial ruin were cushioned with such a generous outpouring of gifts from Nathan's friends near and far. Friends showed up with keto casseroles and gift cards. And teachers from both schools sent care packages full of cards and posters signed by students. Everyone was rooting for his recovery.

Learning to care for Nathan took on a new dimension as he adjusted to life in the house in a wheelchair, with only the use of his non-dominant hand. We had to communicate each move we made, working in tandem to transition him from the chair to the bed, the couch, the toilet, or to sit on the shower bench. He was relieved to be home but growing angry at his inability to do things for himself.

Not only was his brain recovering from trauma, but his body, which he had always taken care of, was atrophying with the lack of use. Still, he wanted to do every single thing that he could for himself, and if I jumped in to help, he would yell at me: "I want to do it for myself until I can't anymore." I couldn't blame him. But I also knew—that time had already come.

One of the biggest side effects of hemiplegia—the paralyzation of one vertical half of your body—we had to contend with was incontinence. Because half of his body didn't work, the little internal sensor that tells your brain you need to empty your bladder stopped working as well. When he sensed he had to go, it was too late in a matter of seconds. After many rounds of changing underwear and clothes, we devised a bell system. He'd ring it, and I would drop whatever I was doing and come running with a plastic pitcher. There was no time to make our way to the bathroom. And none of the urinals we had bought worked well. My friend told us about the plastic pitcher hack, and it worked best. I brought up the idea of an external catheter, and that was met with a resounding, "Hell no, over my dead body," so I dropped it. Sleep was scarce. My life revolved around Nathan's need to urinate. The bell sent me into an adrenaline-fueled sprint, day or night.

The complexity of our situation was compounded by the notion of toxic positivity. We often felt we had to maintain a positive outlook, even in the face of immense suffering. This pressure to stay perpetually optimistic felt suffocating at times. It invalidated the very real pain, fear, and grief that we were experiencing. It became increasingly clear that acknowledging and expressing these emotions was not only necessary but healthy.

This chapter of our lives taught me that it's okay to not be okay. Hope and despair can coexist, and true strength lies in facing our reality, no matter how daunting it may be. It highlighted the need for a support system that acknowledges the suffering and offers genuine, compassionate understanding—a safe space where one can be vulnerable without the fear of judgment or the pressure of unwavering positivity.

LET'S CHECK IN

For readers in similar situations, navigating the complexities of a loved one's illness, it's essential to recognize the duality of such experiences. There is the profound love and connection that deepens in the face of hardship, but there's also the personal toll it takes. It's a constant balancing act between supporting your loved one and taking care of your own well-being, between hope and realism, and between fighting and accepting.

In such times, it's crucial to acknowledge and respect your feelings, seeking support when necessary (I know it's easier said than done). It's about finding strength in vulnerability, understanding that it's okay to feel overwhelmed, and recognizing the importance of self-care. These physical battles against illness demand emotional and psychological resilience from everyone involved.

It's okay to feel overwhelmed. It's okay to have days when you can't keep it together. It's in these moments that we discover our capacity for love and our strength in vulnerability. Although you may not recognize it until much later, you're learning, growing, and evolving. You will get through this.

In early moments of shock during trauma, it can be helpful to do the following:

Pause and breathe: It sounds simple, but taking a moment to pause and focus on your breathing can be incredibly powerful.

When overwhelmed, our breath often becomes shallow, which can increase anxiety and stress. By taking deep, controlled breaths, you activate your body's natural relaxation response. This can be a quick way to center yourself. Try inhaling deeply for a count of three to five seconds, holding for a count of the same, and then exhaling for a count of three to five. Repeat this several times until you feel a sense of calm.

Grounding techniques: Use grounding techniques to bring yourself back to the present moment. One effective method is the 5-4-3-2-1 technique.[7] Look around and name five things you can see, four things you can touch, three things you can hear, two things you can smell, and one thing you can taste. This exercise can help distract you from overwhelming thoughts and bring your focus back to your current environment. More simply, sometimes I count backward from 100 and find it engages my logical brain enough to distract me from overwhelming emotion.

Seek immediate support: If the overwhelm feels too intense to manage alone, don't hesitate to reach out for support.

7 "Notice: Mental Health Awareness Month," Weekly Phoenix, Florida Polytechnic University, accessed January 1, 2024, https://weeklyphoenix.floridapoly.edu/notice/mental-health-awareness-month-3/.

When you're facing terrible times, people have a habit of saying some of the most insensitive things while meaning well. In times of adversity, finding solace and strength in words of wisdom can be incredibly powerful. Here are quotes, parables, scriptures, and thoughts that may offer comfort and reflection during challenging times:

The Serenity Prayer by Reinhold Niebuhr:

"God, grant me the serenity to accept the things I cannot change, courage to change the things I can, and wisdom to know the difference."[8]

A Parable of Resilience—The Bamboo and The Oak:

The bamboo bends with the wind, while the oak stands firm. In a storm, the oak may break, but the bamboo sways and survives.

This parable teaches the value of resilience and flexibility in the face of adversity.

Scripture—Psalm 46:1-2:

"God is our refuge and strength, an ever-present help in trouble. Therefore we will not fear, though the earth give way and the mountains fall into the heart of the sea."

---

[8] Lee, K.J., and Robyn M. Smith. "EHR/EMR: "Meaningful Use," Stimulus Money, and the Serenity Prayer." Ear, Nose, & Throat Journal, (2011), accessed January 1, 2024, https://doi.org/10.1177/014556131109000215.

The Parable of the Two Wolves—A Native American Tale:

A Cherokee man tells his grandson about a battle that goes on inside people. He says, "My son, the battle is between two wolves inside us all. One is Evil. It is anger, envy, jealousy, sorrow, regret, greed, arrogance, self-pity, guilt, resentment, inferiority, lies, false pride, superiority, and ego. The other is Good. It is joy, peace, love, hope, serenity, humility, kindness, benevolence, empathy, generosity, truth, compassion, and faith." The grandson thought about it for a minute and then asked his grandfather, "Which wolf wins?" The old Cherokee simply replied, "The one you feed."[9]

Quote by Helen Keller:

"Although the world is full of suffering, it is also full of the overcoming of it."[10]

The Parable of the Farmer and His Horse:

A farmer's horse runs away, and the neighbors say, "What bad luck!" The farmer replies, "Maybe." The next day, the horse returns with three wild horses, and the neighbors say, "What good luck!" The farmer replies, "Maybe." The following day, his son tries to ride one of the wild horses, is thrown, and breaks his leg. The neighbors say, "What bad luck!" The farmer replies, "Maybe." The next week, the

---

[9] Alfaro, Tanya. "Saving the Boys: Anticipating Moral Engagement in Lord of the Flies." (2022), accessed January 1, 2024, https://core.ac.uk/download/526060011.pdf.

[10] "Question Tag: Helen Keller," English Notes, accessed January 1, 2024, https://englishnotes.com/question-tag/helen-keller/.

army comes to conscript young men but passes over the farmer's son due to his broken leg. The neighbors say, "What good luck!" The farmer replies, "Maybe."[11]

This parable teaches that the true nature of events isn't always clear, and what seems like misfortune can turn out to be fortunate.

[11] "Luke 8:4-15, June 10, 2018," Peace Covenant Presbyterian, accessed January 1, 2024, https://www.peacecovenantpckw.com/luke-84-15-june-10-2018/.

6

Facing Death to Truly Live

"Pain looks like a lot of things. You may not recognize it when you see it."

— Terri Guillemets

L et's face it: talking about death is tough. No one wants to think about their own mortality or talk to a loved one about theirs. But here's the thing: avoiding the conversation doesn't make it any less real.

In this final chapter, I share some deeply personal moments of loss, not because I have any answers or solutions, but simply because I believe it's important to talk about it. To be prepared, so that when the inevitable does happen—and it will—we might be able to face it with some sense of understanding.

I've stumbled through this narrative around death more than I'd care to admit, including my own words here. But what I've come to learn is this: it's better to have the conversation than to leave things unsaid. So, let's do this together.

Before Nathan's diagnosis, I had been making monthly trips to visit Mom. She had named me as her POA, and I felt a responsibility to ensure her needs were being taken care of. I did this in consultation with my brother, of course. We agreed it was our priority to keep Mom in her own home for as long as possible, with my brother and new wife offering to take her in at their house if things got too bad. Assessing her needs was a month-to-month process, as her decline would speed up and then slow down. The same person who cared for my grandmother full-time (after my mom got sick and couldn't any longer) offered her services to care for my mom. She would keep my brother and me updated on Mom's condition, and let us know when it was time to bring in more help. Angel, as she was affectionately known, called me one day, shortly after Nathan's surgery. She was crying. She said she absolutely hated to put this on me with everything else we were facing, but Mom had declined to the point we needed to consider placement in a facility. Mom had always called Karen (her actual name) an "Earth Angel." She was indeed that. I used to joke with her that she'd be caring for me next.

She believed a facility—and not my brother's house—was best for Mom. To put the burden of care on a new marriage was not wise, and it wasn't in Mom's best interest. Her needs were unique and growing. I hired a consultant to help me find the right care for her.

A week or so after Nathan came home, the consultant lined up a day of visiting nursing homes in Kingsport, where Mom lived. To be gone for the least amount of time, I left early in the morning for the four-and-a-half-hour trip. My brother met us there, and we toured four or so facilities before I made the trip back. It took eighteen hours in all. And it was an emotional visit. My brother still wanted him and his wife to take Mom into their home and care for her. The consultant and I were advocating for her to go to a facility designed for her care. As POA, I had the ultimate decision, but I wanted my brother to agree and be okay with it.

Obviously, I didn't want my mom to go to a nursing home, either. More than anything, I wanted my mom back. I wanted to be able to talk to her every night. I longed for the days when my mom was just a phone call away. I wanted her to tell me I was a good mom and wife, and that my life wasn't over. But now I had to let all that go. It was too late. Nothing mattered anymore. A bone-deep depression took hold of me, and for the first time in my life, I was not a functioning person with anxiety. I was experiencing the immobilization of depression. Unless I was seeing to Nathan's needs, I was otherwise in bed, asleep, or listening to depressing music. I could muster no energy for anything else. I longed for someone to save me from what I was feeling. It required an inner strength I wasn't sure I possessed, and I lacked small acts of self-care and self-compassion. I had no promise of better days to come.

I decided I would see my doctor about my depression. I knew the answer would be to go on medication. It was the first time in my life I would take mood-regulating meds, and I had tried to avoid it. It was a big step, and I cried while making the appointment, in the car on the way to the office, and throughout the entire visit. It was embarrassing. But without the meds, I knew I couldn't control it.

The road to finding the right medication wasn't easy. It was a trial-and-error process. But with each passing day, I began to feel a shift. It was subtle at first, like the first rays of dawn gently piercing through the night. Gradually, the medication began to allow me to function again.

To you, who might be facing a similar struggle, know that seeking medical help and considering medication is not a sign of weakness, and it's not something to be scared of exploring. It is a brave step towards self-care and healing. It's about giving yourself permission to use all available resources to find your way back to wellness. I don't know why it took me so long to embrace this truth.

I had planned a big birthday celebration at East Nashville Beer Works for Nathan's 53rd birthday. But a couple of weeks before, I had seen a rapid decline in him. One day, I arrived at school to pick him up, and his pants were soiled. Instead of calling me, he sat in his urine at school for half a day. I told Nathan it was time—way past time—for him to stop working. He finally agreed and notified his principal. I cannot imagine the helplessness he felt that day, knowing he would never return, knowing how hard he had tried to continue working.

On the day of his party, I was concerned he wasn't well enough to make the trip in the car to the venue. He was in extreme pain. Somehow, he rallied and put on one of the best performances of his life. We were surrounded by our community and our friends for an entire afternoon. A friend had baked and donated Hulk-themed cookies for the party, and other friends had purchased a button maker and enlisted the students in the kids' classes to make "Team Davis" buttons they passed out at the party and at school. A friend said to Nathan, "Isn't it so cool that all these people are here for you?" And Nathan looked at him and said, "They're not here for me. They're here for each other."

It was such a Nathan thing to say. He valued the importance of community so much and spent most of his time building and fostering community. He knew that they were indeed there just as much to strengthen each other as they were to encourage Nathan to keep fighting.

Just before Nathan's party, we had another ER visit after a seizure. The MRI they gave him showed us that the inevitable was happening. The tumors had grown and spread, and there was really no looking back. I'll never forget the doctors coming into our room, going over the scan, and saying, "What do you want us to do?" Knowing full well there was really nothing they could do, we couldn't really come up with anything either. The empty, hopeless feeling was too heavy.

After the party, Nathan's neurosurgeon friend and his wife sat at our kitchen table. Nathan was already asleep, worn out from the party. I brought up the pictures of the scan and handed Anthony my phone. "How much time do you think he has left?" I hesitated to ask him. I felt like things had only been going downhill, but no one had told me to make any changes—like stopping treatment or calling hospice. He said that the monster was growing at a neck-breaking pace, and based on scans he'd seen throughout his experience, Nathan had about six weeks left. He told me I needed to talk to Nathan about shifting gears ASAP.

"Call hospice today," he told me.

I already knew from previous conversations that Nathan didn't want to know any end-of-life timelines like this. So that evening, I sat next to his bed and talked about the benefits of hospice, including a hospital bed and special equipment to make managing his care easier. He agreed, and hospice workers and equipment arrived within a couple of days. February 14, 2020, to be exact. Valentine's Day.

One of the biggest benefits hospice brought to us was talking about death. Sitting in our living room that day, we began talking about the inevitable. While it was as depressing as it sounds, it was also a huge relief.

The blend of days and nights, the palliative care, and the final moments in hospice are etched deeply in my memory. The finality of his passing, though somewhat expected, hit with an unanticipated force. It left me in a state of introspection about life, death, and the journey in between.

They say death isn't linear. It's more of a back-and-forth process of leaving the body and returning. In the couple of weeks at home before his death, Nathan often didn't know where he was. He would ask me, or I would ask him. Most of the time he thought he was in the hospital—probably because he was in a hospital bed.

Sometimes, he called me Jan, which is his sister's name. One morning, he told me he left home and had just gotten back. I knew we were near the end when he said this. Every day, friends came to visit. He always rallied for these visits and did his best to smile, tell a joke, and stay alert while they were there.

Friends flew in from different parts of the country. Local friends came, took pictures, and said the most hopeful goodbyes they could muster. A longtime friend asked what she could bring, and I told her cookies for his sweet tooth. She brought a box full of enormous bakery-style cookies, each one as big as his face. Nathan lay there and ate them one by one while she and I talked. We laughed and wondered how his body was even able to contain them. He was thin and emaciated, like those who are approaching death.

Nathan had been completely bed-bound for a couple of weeks, and sleeping for greater stretches at a time. At least twice a day, he would wake up, assume it was morning, and ask for coffee with peanut butter and honey toast. He had long given up on keto, and I did my best to give him foods he enjoyed. But this was his go-to. I would laugh when he would request his "breakfast" in the evening and thought it was so bittersweet that Nathan was doubling his last days by having two mornings a day.

Hospice felt like very little help at all in the day-to-day. Someone would come by each day for fifteen minutes, ask some questions, and leave. They would tell me he was declining. They couldn't tell me how much time we had left.

His pain was increasing, and hospice had given me a box full of special medications to administer. I would give him liquid morphine via a mouth syringe about once a day, but sometimes it wouldn't be enough, especially with the growing headaches. He increasingly made very little sense when he talked. It seemed he had a form of aphasia, not unlike my mother.

March 3, 2020, a strong storm ripped through Nashville, unleashing tornados and devastation in our neighborhood of East Nashville (and across Middle Tennessee). I was panicked about what to do when the storm hit. I couldn't move Nathan from his hospital bed. I hunkered down in the tornado closet with the kids the best I could until it passed. Our area was spared from damage, and thankfully, Nathan had slept through it all.

Our beloved community was hard hit, though. The historic church building where Rowan had been attending a youth group had been destroyed, and her youth pastor was also in the process of transitioning out to another job. Loss surrounded us.

Nathan was never conscious enough to know about the tornado, and his body began to slowly shut down. That Friday, the staff from his school came to visit, and Nathan was unable to make sense or understand what was going on. I felt bad I had allowed them to visit, because it was undoubtedly traumatic for them, but I didn't realize that day would be the beginning of the end.

The next morning, Nathan began vomiting. Because he was bed-bound, and the vomiting had taken me by surprise, I had to change his bedding and chuck pad when he threw up. He vomited again forty-five minutes later, and I repeated the process, quickly washing and drying the extra set of linens. I sat by his bed, ready with the trash can when the heaving would start again. I tried the nausea medication, but it wasn't working. I did this for hours. At one point, I was on the back side of the bed, changing his bedding, when he began to vomit again. Afraid of him choking, I jumped up on the bed, standing and straddling his body to grab the trash can and push his head to the side to keep him from aspirating. I yelled to Rowan for help because I couldn't reach the trash can. She walked in, saw me standing over the bed, him vomiting, dirty bed sheets hanging off. She gave me the trash can with eyes so big, and I remember thinking this was too much for her to see. I knew at that moment I could no longer try to keep him home until the end. I couldn't stop him from vomiting. I couldn't manage his pain. I had to have help.

When he was resting again, I walked out the front porch and called the hospice number, crying.

"I can't do it anymore," I sobbed.

They assured me it was okay, and that they would send a crew within a couple of hours to transport him to an in-patient hospice downtown.

The next day, I made my way to Nathan's room at the hospice. He stopped eating the morning before he was transferred. He slept mostly, and I noticed the nurses had placed an internal catheter. His head was still leaning acutely to one side, almost as if he was still in pain. Nurses gave him pain medicine only as needed and no more than every four to six hours.

Sitting there, in hospice, was like an alternative universe. It was the first time I didn't have something to do—no sheets to change, no spills to clean up. I watched for any sign of him waking, and I took his face in my hands and coached him.

I told him later, "You got this. I'm so proud of you. You're my hero."

He responded weakly and said, "You're a good kisser."

His eyes closed again.

I asked the doctor the next day if they would let me know when would be the last time we could talk to him because I wanted to make sure the kids had an opportunity to say goodbye. "Well, I suggest you do it now," he said.

Seconds later, my phone rang. It was the kids' school counselor, Isla. She asked if there was anything I needed, anything she could do. I couldn't believe the timing. I relayed what the doctor said and asked if she could bring the kids. She said absolutely. She exuded a calm confidence that made me believe she could walk on water. Less than an hour later, she arrived with the kids. Nathan roused enough for them to talk to him, and a friend took some pictures as we shared final moments together.

Isla sat with the kids and helped them do some activities. Emmeline drew Daddy a picture that we hung on the wall with other decorations friends had made, and Rowan wrote him a letter. She knew he wouldn't be able to read it, but the counselor encouraged her to write it. it would be good for her. I later found this letter stuffed between the cushions of the couch in the hospice room. I read it with tears streaming down my face. How does a child say goodbye to her father?

Friends who had supported us so amazingly throughout the sickness organized a parade of care. I was rarely without someone in the room with us. They brought food, coffee, and the gift of presence.

I was okay with the fact that Nathan wasn't going to be able to die at home. I knew that his wish was to not be in pain, and I felt like he would have better palliative care in the hands of the professionals. The hospice room was dimly lit, just a dated-looking lamp on a nightstand next to a recliner. Days and nights blurred together, and I never wanted to leave. I would walk down the hall to the breakroom to warm up coffee, and I'd pick up snippets of news programs about the growing concern over the COVID pandemic.

I felt insulated from the world, and kind of grateful to be in this dark bubble.

I played the classic rock station on the TV monitor overhead. I was observing Nathan's journey from this life to the next.

The next day, Nathan's body posture completely changed. He didn't seem to be tense with pain. His body was relaxed, though he was still unconscious. We were told that hearing is the last to go, so we should be mindful and intentional with conversation in the room. In retrospect, I don't know that I did this to the degree that I wish I had.

Nurses would check a couple of times a day for changes in status. They would explain they were looking for mottling on his feet and ragged breathing. I was concerned he wasn't eating or drinking, but they explained the body no longer wants these things during this phase. His lips were constantly dry, so I'd rub Vaseline on them with a Q-Tip and sometimes my finger. It was the only job I had left.

Friends encouraged me to go home for a shower and a break. Nurses reminded me that loved ones often wait to go when they're alone. I didn't want Nathan to be alone, but I admitted that I needed the rest. I began leaving him at night and would come back the next day. Thursday afternoon, Nathan's friend, who is a barber, came and gave him a final shave. It felt like a holy act of preparing a body for burial and was a fitting tribute for a guy who put great care into his appearance.

That weekend, I watched as his breathing changed and became labored. I read about end-of-life breathing patterns and counted the frequency. This had to be it. His feet were mottled. All the signs were there, but his heart and lungs were so healthy and strong, the doctor would say after her morning rounds. Our friends would remark about how strong he was and how long he was holding out. We believed he'd go on his own terms. We talked lightheartedly about this, but it was stressful. I didn't want him to continue suffering.

Sunday, the eighth day in hospice, the nurse asked me if I was okay with increasing his dosage of Dilaudid (an opioid eight times stronger than morphine) to every hour in an effort to relax his breathing, which was still labored and mechanical. It wasn't until much later I realized this high dosage of narcotics was actually the thing that killed him—a compassionate act of assisted death. Maybe it was an unspoken practice among hospice nurses who watch patients and their families labor through the dying process. I didn't know at the time, but since then, I've heard this is true. I just knew that after all the waiting, I was still unprepared for the finality of death.

I wasn't there when he died. I had gotten a call that afternoon as I sat in his room. It was from a care associate at Mom's facility. A weekend worker had given Mom a piece of pecan pie, and she has an anaphylactic allergy to tree nuts.

I still had her EpiPen in my garage with the boxes from her house, and they didn't have any on-site. I, of course, felt immediate guilt over this. They had called an ambulance and asked me to meet her in the ER, as no one from the facility would be with her. Not wanting Nathan to be alone, I called a friend and asked if they could come over as soon as possible to be with him. They told me they were on their way.

Mom cried when she saw me. She was confused and scared. But physically, she was fine. I wondered if she had even ingested any nuts. Then she was happy just to spend time with me. She begged me not to take her back.

Friends told me Nathan's breathing remained mechanical and labored, and he was unconscious. They talked to him and assured him they'd take care of the kids and me. Another couple came to relieve them. They sang hymns and read from the book of Psalms. I knew he was in good hands, and I was exhausted after getting Mom back to the facility. I questioned whether to even go back to hospice that evening.

I was ten minutes away when I got a call from the hospice nurse. "I'm sorry to inform you your husband has just passed away." I had barely left him over the eight days he'd been at hospice. Every time he seemed to rouse, I would be right there, my hands cupping the sides of his face, telling him how good he was doing, that I was there, and how much I loved him. I was so proud of him.

When Dan and Sara walked out that afternoon, he took his last breath. After I got the call, I called them. They asked if I wanted them to come back and be with me, and I said yes.

I walked into the room. His skin color had turned yellowish-green and looked taut. Tears came immediately as I bent over to rub his chest and face and kiss his forehead again and again. My purse strap slid off my shoulder, and my purse banged into the hospital bed. I looked up and Dan and Sara were there, by my side. Sara took my purse.

I stroked his head and tried to memorize his hairline, knowing it was the last time I'd see it. Of all things, that was the detail I was desperate to remember. All those years it had been right in front of me, and I had never bothered to look at the individual hairs, which had recently grown back from the rounds of radiation. I knew this body that I had lived with for sixteen-plus years would soon be a pile of ashes. This familiar body whose presence I had so taken for granted would soon be destroyed. I told Sara it was probably best I didn't dwell. She agreed. I hugged them and cried into their shoulders, then squared up and wiped my face. My next job was to tell the kids.

I walked down the hallway to meet Julie, who had been keeping the kids and brought them to hospice. A hospice worker opened the library for us. All the common areas had been shut down due to growing concerns about the spread of COVID. There was also a minimum number of visitors per patient, but they had waived this limitation just for us. The hallway began to fill with our closest friends who had labored with us night and day during the last week.

I sat down with the kids and told them, while choking back tears, "I'm so sorry. Your Daddy passed away." This was the single worst moment of my life. We all held each other crying. There was nothing else to do or feel. No hopeful messages of recovery to cling to. This was final and irreversible. It was just the three of us now. And while Daddy's suffering had ended, it seemed to be a big shock to the children. I felt I hadn't prepared them for this reality. Julie wrapped her arms around us and began to pray for our comfort and peace.

After a few minutes, we walked to the hallway outside of his room and hugged the necks of our friends. They asked what I wanted them to do, if I wanted them to come over. I said yes, and that evening we had pizza and wine.

Julie refused to leave us alone through the next day, but as the immediate shock and fog lifted, news of the pandemic began to sink in. Nathan died on March 15, 2020—the same week the shelter-at-home order began. A sense of fear and panic began to set in, and I told Julie she should stay at home. The kids and I would hunker down until this all passed. We'd be okay.

It was a strange and heartbreaking take on death when I had to see and handle Nathan's personal effects after he passed. His glasses, hat, keys—these were things that I would've seen him use often, so being able to hold them felt very surreal. Even though his body was absent, the familiarity of these well-worn items still spoke volumes.

Quite overwhelmed and unsure of what I should do with them, I decided to store them in a drawer for safekeeping. It made me realize that death wouldn't involve big dramatic moments from here on out; instead, death would be seen and felt through everyday things. It came too suddenly and sadly, but all that remained were those small bits of him—powerful reminders of a husband, father, son, and brother.

In the quiet aftermath of Nathan's passing, I found myself grappling with the harsh reality of finality. Despite all the preparation, the end still arrived with a suddenness that left me reeling. The final goodbye was a moment I had anticipated in countless ways, yet when it unfolded, it was nothing like I had imagined. The permanence of loss struck me with a force that was both overwhelming and deeply sobering.

Now, four years later, as I face the reality of preparing to say goodbye to my mom, who recently entered hospice care, I can't help but feel a mix of emotions. It's a bittersweet time, reminding me of the deep connection we've always shared. She was my first sanctuary, right from the start in her womb, and that's a bond that's pretty hard to shake.

Thinking about those early days, before I even entered the world, it occurs to me that it was the safest place possible, surrounded by the steady rhythm of her heartbeat. Now, as we're entering this final phase, I'm filled with gratitude. Mom has always been a pillar in my life, from my earliest memories to now. She's been my guide, my support, and my constant source of strength. And in this chapter of our lives, I find myself stepping into a new role, offering her the comfort and security she once gave me.

In the end, the finality of death is a profound truth that each of us must face in our own way. In recognizing and honoring that we're here temporarily, our sanctuary allows us to live more fully, embracing each moment with greater depth and mindfulness. It teaches us to cherish our connections, celebrate our joys, and face our sorrows with a heart that appreciates the preciousness of time. Can you imagine arriving at death with a sense of peace as a result of living so fully? May we learn the art of living and dying with grace. May we embrace the full spectrum of our human experience and find beauty and meaning in both our beginnings and our endings.

For so long death has been a part of my life, something I feared, and that made me feel unsafe. When I learned to embrace death as part of life, I came to terms with the reality it presents for us all. By accepting death, I tapped into my inner sanctuary—a safe haven from the difficult realities and an invaluable source of strength when times are tough. This experience made me reflect on the broader concept of being a sanctuary for others.

The greatest gift of a sanctuary is its ability to offer comfort and protection to those in need. When I was growing up in the church, we referred to the auditorium as the "the sanctuary." I imagine this is a common moniker in the South or among fundamentalist churches, but clearly, the metaphor stuck with me. A sanctuary is a holy, set-apart space. Because of that, there were special rules, especially for children and especially during services: no unnecessary trips in and out, no gum-chewing, no chit-chat. The sanctuary was meant to be a safe space for connecting with the divine.

The notion of a sanctuary as a holy and set-apart space, where reverence and respect are paramount, translates beautifully into everyday life.

In sanctuary, my love didn't have to be never-ending and constant. It could be fragile and vulnerable and human. In fact, I could choose to be all those things as a mother, friend, daughter, and sister. I could choose to sit with anxiety, ask forgiveness when needed, and seek connection and help. And I, in turn, could do the same for the people who love me. Taking turns to shelter; to lift the heavy burdens; to share in joy, pain, and sorrow ... until death do us all part, and we're finally whole and safe.

LET'S CHECK IN

In the sanctuary of our minds, we sometimes need external help to restore balance. Medication can be a powerful ally in this journey, offering a helping hand when our own strength falters. It's okay to lean on this support, to allow it to guide you back to a place where you can stand on your own again.

Remember, seeking help is a courageous act, a testament to your commitment to your well-being. It's a choice that honors your need for support in a time of vulnerability. So, if you find yourself in the shadow of depression or anxiety, consider reaching out for medical help. It could be the first step towards a brighter, more hopeful path.

Taking medication for mental health is as valid and necessary as taking medication for any physical health condition. Here are five ways in which medication makes a difference:[12]

Restores chemical balance: Many mental health issues, such as depression and anxiety, are linked to chemical imbalances in the brain. Medications can help restore this balance, alleviating symptoms and improving overall mood and function.

Reduces symptoms: Medication can significantly reduce the severity of symptoms associated with mental health disorders. This can

---

[12] "5 Benefits of Medication Management," Greater Lowell Psychiatric Associates, accessed January 1, 2024, https://www.greaterlowellpsychassoc.com/blog/5-benefits-of-medication-management.

include lessening feelings of sadness or hopelessness in depression, reducing excessive worry in anxiety, or stabilizing mood swings in bipolar disorder.

Improves daily functioning: By managing symptoms effectively, medication can enhance your ability to function in daily life. This can mean better performance at work, improved relationships, and a greater ability to engage in social activities and hobbies.

Supports therapy: Medication can be especially effective when used with therapy. It can provide a level of symptom relief that allows you to engage in therapeutic processes more effectively and develop coping strategies.

Prevents relapse: For many, medication can help prevent relapse of symptoms. Continual use, as prescribed by a healthcare professional, can provide ongoing support and stability.

It's okay to acknowledge the pain and the heartache of loss while cherishing the love and memories that remain. If you're facing similar challenges, know that it's okay to feel overwhelmed and to seek moments of respite, however fleeting they may be. In this season, we find our strength not in denial, but in embracing the full spectrum of our human experience.

Acknowledge the suffering, the fear, and the uncertainty. Admit that hope sometimes feels distant, that the relentless positivity of others can feel suffocating. Find spaces where you can be honest about your feelings and where you can express your fears without judgment.

Above all, remember that your resilience, your ability to keep going in the face of overwhelming challenges, is a testament to the depth of your love and commitment.

Sometimes, challenges to our emotional and mental well-being manifest subtly. They creep into our daily lives almost unnoticed. It's crucial to periodically pause and reflect on your mental health status. Here are five questions to ask yourself and honestly answer:

- Do you often feel overwhelmed by your responsibilities?
- Have you noticed changes in your mood, behavior, or interest in doing things?
- Are you experiencing physical symptoms like fatigue, insomnia, changes in appetite, or even nerve pain?
- Do you feel that you don't have a good support system of friends, family, or community to meet your emotional and mental needs?
- Do you find it hard to engage in self-care or self-compassion activities because you're just surviving?

Recognizing the signs that you might need help is a critical step toward taking care of your mental health. This self-assessment is not a diagnostic tool but rather a means to encourage mindfulness about your mental well-being. If you find yourself answering yes to most of the above questions, it may be an indication that seeking professional guidance could be beneficial.

We don't talk about death enough as a society. Death, in many cultures, remains a taboo topic, often shrouded in fear and avoidance. However, embracing death as a natural part of life can help us approach life more fully and prepare for the eventual loss of others we love.

Here are some ways to approach the subject of death in a healthy and constructive way:

Open conversation: Encourage open discussions about death with family and friends. This can demystify the subject and help dispel any fears or misconceptions. Contemplating our mortality can be a powerful exercise in understanding the fragility and preciousness of life. This can be a helpful exercise for people like me who struggle to stay present in the moment.

Prepare for the inevitable: Consider practical aspects such as wills, funeral plans, and end-of-life care. Preparing for these eventualities can bring peace of mind and help ease the burden on loved ones. Consider software like everplans.com to help you think through what you need.

Support systems: Seek out or create support systems for dealing with grief and loss. Community groups, online forums, or therapy can provide valuable spaces for sharing and healing. For cancer victims and their families, Gilda's Club offers valuable free resources, including social and emotional support groups.

For those who might find themselves on a similar path, here are some insights and tips that I gleaned from my experience:

Allow yourself to feel: It's essential to let yourself experience the full range of emotions that come with loss. Grief, anger, relief, guilt, and even moments of peace can all be part of your journey. Embrace them without judgment.

Create a ritual: Rituals, whether public or private, can provide a sense of closure. This could be a memorial service, a personal goodbye, or a simple act such as lighting a candle or writing to your loved one. In the months after her father passed, I found that my youngest daughter had texted her dad's number to say that she missed him. It ripped my heart open, but I also appreciated what a practical and creative way she found to process her grief.

Preserve memories: Find ways to honor and remember your loved one through creating a photo album, planting a tree, or simply sharing stories about them with others.

Be patient with yourself: There is no timeline for grieving. Allow yourself to move through this process at your own pace. Some days will be harder than others, and that's perfectly normal.

Embrace change: The loss will inevitably bring changes to your life. Embrace them as part of your new reality. It's okay to start new traditions or routines that suit your changed circumstances.

Plan for tough moments: Birthdays, anniversaries, and holidays can be particularly challenging. Plan ahead for how you'll spend these days. Sometimes, just having a plan can ease the anxiety of these milestones.

How can you embrace the idea of sanctuary in your life? Consider the roles you play—each presents an opportunity to be a sanctuary for yourself or someone else. For example, as a parent, the sanctuary you provide might be one of unconditional love, stability, and guidance. For a friend, it might mean being a reliable confidante or a source of comfort during tough times. In your community, acting as a sanctuary could involve volunteering, advocating for those who are marginalized, or simply being a kind and respectful presence.

Ask yourself: *In what ways can I provide support and safety to those around me?* Embrace the idea of being a sanctuary for others and make a conscious effort to be a supportive presence in the lives of those around you. Creating space—whether physical or emotional—enriches the lives of others and adds depth and purpose to our own.

Also ask yourself: *In what ways can I provide support and safety to myself?* This is the most profound form of sanctuary.

Grief and Courage

The pandemic was a mixed bag for me and my kids, as I'm sure it was for most people. Over the first few months of the lockdown, my kids and I felt a sense of isolation from our community. All the while, bad memories lurked in every shadowy corner of our "sunny" house. Deep scrapes from Nathan's wheelchair scarred the walls and the doorways. We were spending ALL our time at home with nowhere to go.

We began to dream about what it might look like to move to a different house with more land, perhaps with some chickens running around. It was a Pinterest-fueled cottage core fantasy, and it was just enough motivation to begin driving around looking at houses and mini farms for sale. We justified this as a COVID-safe activity.

It was all conjecture until one drive put us in front of an old house on a few acres of land. I wondered if we could really live in such a dreamy house. It looked like it came straight out of Southern Living magazine. I began to envision all the things we could do—from hosting family movie nights to picnics on the lawn. I believe Nathan would have loved this house as much as we did. I could picture him riding on his motorcycle through the winding, hilly roads leading to the farm.

Perhaps it was time for something new. But we weren't throwing out the old completely. I certainly couldn't sell the house that I had already bought twice. Our good friends moved into our old house to rent and take care of it while we explored and wrote new chapters of our story. Here on the hilltop, we would have room to heal, grow, and expand. We would learn to be a family of three and discover how to open our hearts to more life, embracing the possibilities around every corner. Over our mantle was a wooden sign that read, "Every family has a story … " We continued to write ours every day.

At night, I could hear an army of frogs around the koi pond that flanked our front porch. I imagined a miniature band of bluegrass amphibians taking to the sidewalk with a tiny banjo and an upright bass, singing songs passed down to them from the time they were tadpoles. Some of them wore caps, others tweed vests, but all of them were committed to singing a plucky, boisterous tune in the night for a gathered audience of crickets, beetles, and field mice to pass the time. But only when humans were out of sight.

Maybe all this isolation during COVID had my imagination running wild. But speaking of anthropomorphizing animals, I was exploring my identity as a Taurus, the bull, which is an earth sign. I wasn't exactly sure what that meant, except that I was discovering how much I loved to play in the dirt. This was definitely a first for someone unaccustomed to having dirt under her nails. There was no shortage of work on the mini farm. From the chickens to gardening to weeding to mowing with my badass, top-of-the-line John Deere riding lawn mower. And that was just the outside.

Inside, I undertook what became a year-long project to renovate the interior with fresh paint and decor and—the most ambitious undertaking of all—finish out the enormous basement. When I say enormous, it felt like an entirely other world down there. The basement/garage combo not only encompassed the footprint of the house but extended under the wraparound porch as well, looking out into the descending lush forested hillside.

This entire place represented something new for us—a new season, starting over, starting fresh. Artist and writer Mary Anne Radmacher said, "Courage doesn't always roar. Sometimes courage is the quiet voice at the end of the day saying, 'I will try again tomorrow.'"[13] I didn't feel particularly energetic or motivated in this season. I was still napping a lot. But I kept getting up every day and committing to trying something new.

The idea of "something new" stuck with me, and I began to refer to the mini farm as Something New Farm. Everything about this season was new for me. Buying a home by myself. Caring for the land and the house. Raising chickens (and for a brief, terrible time, ducklings). Growing food, finishing a basement, and including space

[13] Mary Anne Radmacher. Goodreads. https://www.goodreads.com/author/quotes/149829.Mary_Anne_Radmacher.

that held the potential for lots of gatherings. I didn't believe this was about throwing out the old. I believed it was about embracing seasons and the cyclical nature of life. Just as a new moon is packed with meaning, when it's darkest, change is most possible.

If you find yourself in a similar season, remember that moving forward doesn't always require grand leaps. Sometimes, it's about the small steps, the quiet decisions to keep going, and the soft whisper of courage that guides you through each day. Whether you're dealing with loss, facing a new challenge, or simply finding your way in a changed world, know that your strength lies in your ability to try again, day after day.

Living in sanctuary doesn't mean being free from fear, anxiety, or shame. Rather, it means acknowledging these emotions as part of our human experience, yet not allowing them to imprison us or blind us to the beauty and potential that life holds.

In fact, I want to share a secret with you. This book you hold was not the one I originally intended to publish. In a moment of over-whelming shame and despair, I discarded the earlier version—a raw, unfiltered outpouring of my inner turmoil. It was a book written for myself, a necessary step in my healing journey. In keeping it for myself, I found liberation and the courage to start anew. I crafted this new version with the intention that it would be of more help to others who might find themselves in similar seasons of pain.

One of my former freelance clients was a big fan of Viktor Frankl, and he often talked about the importance of finding meaning in suffering. He said that after one story of our life climaxes and ends, we feel a deep sense of heaviness. When one story is over, we have to figure something out that we can do next. He paraphrased Frankl and said that to experience a life of meaning, you need: a project to work on, a redemptive perspective on your suffering, and a community of people who love you.[14]

Allison Fallon, a writing coach, said, "It is by giving language to your pain that you transform it into power; and this is how we set ourselves free."[15] Like the little girl who was afraid to get her hands or tights dirty, or like the time I lived among the spiders in exile in the little green house, I had to face all that was wrong on the inside before I could become whole on the outside. I began seeing my therapist again to unpack all of this and told her the contents of what would become this book (in all of its drafts). She encouraged me to make a list of things to "heal" and a list of things to "bring to life." I encourage you to do the same.

As you grapple with your own fears, anxieties, or the weight of shame, remember that these emotions, while powerful, do not define you. They may loom large and ominous at times, but they are not the sum total of who you are. You are a vibrant being, capable of experiencing a vast spectrum of emotions and experiences. To live in sanctuary is to recognize and accept these parts of yourself, and then, gently, to let them go.

---

[14] Viktor E. Frankl et al, *Man's Search for Meaning*. (Boston, Mass: Beacon Press, 2006), 145-46.
[15] Allison Fallon, Twitter post, March 24, 2022, 2:29 P.M. https://twitter.com/missallyfallon/status/1507077099240185856.

Acknowledgments

I'd like to give special thanks to:

My therapist, Cresson, who knows my story better than anyone else and held space for me to unravel it.

My two editors, Aly Hawkins (who also helped write two chapters of an early draft) and Shawn Smucker, who helped me take this book from idea to fruition.

The dedicated editorial team at Transcendent Publishing, publisher Shanda Trofe and editor Clare Fernández, who worked tirelessly on multiple drafts to make my words better.

My children, who are my entire world, for allowing me to tell my version of history and include them in it.

Our Inglewood family, for carrying us in our darkest moments.

Taylor, who helped me find myself.

Maya, who supported me unconditionally.

Chasity and Scott, who helped me pick up the pieces and move forward.

Mom, for being an unmovable source of strength and inspiration.

Jeff, for loving me.

Discover Your Sanctuary Within

Discover "The Sanctuary Within: Empowering Practices for Healing, Resilience, and Embracing Life After Loss" workbook—a free guide that will empower you in your season of healing and embracing life after loss. Download this free workbook now to foster your inner strength and sanctuary amidst the challenges of grief.

"The Sanctuary Within" offers a blend of empowering practices, writing prompts, and exercises crafted to guide you through the healing process. This workbook serves as a compassionate companion, providing comfort and support as you navigate the complexities of grief and loss.

Inside "The Sanctuary Within," you will:

- Engage in reflective exercises that promote healing and self-awareness
- Explore empowering practices to embrace life after loss and find renewed purpose
- Find suggestions for self-care rituals that nourish your mind, body, and soul
- Harness the transformative power of gratitude, mindfulness, and self-compassion

This free workbook is a valuable resource for anyone seeking guidance, support, and inspiration on their healing journey. Whether you are personally experiencing loss, supporting a loved one through grief, or simply yearning to deepen your understanding of the human experience, "The Sanctuary Within" will help you find comfort and embrace the goodness of life.

**Download "The Sanctuary Within" workbook now
at papertiger.store.**

About the Author

Cara Baker is an award-winning writer whose journey began on the launch team for a faith-based media company, where she served as Editorial Director for six years. Within those formative years, she embarked on a mission to empower women, giving birth to a magazine and podcast dedicated to celebrating the strength and resilience of the female spirit. Through her approach to storytelling, Cara helped reshape the landscape of the Christian publishing world and develop the careers of many bestselling authors.

Her work has appeared in *HuffPost*, *New York Post*, and *CNN*. She's also been a source for *USA Today* and *The New York Times*.

Armed with a journalism degree and a master's in digital marketing and analytics, Cara's dedication to the art of storytelling led her back to her educational roots. Currently serving as Director of Digital Communications at her alma mater, she helps build community while paying homage to her family's legacy in the field of education. It is within this sanctuary of learning that she continues to weave narratives that inspire, inform, and spark meaningful conversations.

In her community of East Nashville with her two children, Cara enjoys live music and supporting local businesses. Through her website, Paper Tiger Books, Cara invites readers into a world where vulnerability is embraced, resilience is celebrated, and the power of storytelling holds the key to unlocking profound human connections.

Connect with her at papertiger.store.